Modern Critical Interpretations

William Shakespeare's
Henry IV, Part 1

Modern Critical Interpretations

These and other titles in preparation

Modern Critical Interpretations

William Shakespeare's
Henry IV, Part 1

Edited and with an introduction by

Harold Bloom
Sterling Professor of the Humanities
Yale University

Chelsea House Publishers ◇ 1987
NEW YORK ◇ NEW HAVEN ◇ PHILADELPHIA

© 1987 by Chelsea House Publishers, a division of Chelsea
House Educational Communications, Inc.
   133 Christopher Street, New York, NY 10014
   345 Whitney Avenue, New Haven, CT 06511
   5014 West Chester Pike, Edgemont, PA 19028

Introduction © 1987 by Harold Bloom

Printed and bound in the United States of America

∞ The paper used in this publication meets the minimum
requirements of the American National Standard for
Permanence of Paper for Printed Library Materials,
Z39.48–1984.

Library of Congress Cataloging-in-Publication Data
William Shakespeare's Henry IV, Part 1.
   (Modern critical interpretations)
   Bibliography: p.
   Includes index.
   1. Shakespeare, William, 1564–1616. King Henry IV.
Part 1.   2. Henry IV, King of England, 1367–1413, in
fiction, drama, poetry, etc.   I. Bloom, Harold.   II. Series.
PR2810.W5   1986   822.3'3   86-17600
ISBN 0-87754-925-7

Contents

Editor's Note

This volume gathers together what I judge to be the best criticism of Shakespeare's *Henry IV, Part 1* that has been published during the past thirty-five years, reprinted here in the chronological order of its original publication. I am grateful to Marena Fisher for her aid in editing this book.

My introduction is a celebration of the greatness of Falstaff as a representation, still unique partly because Shakespeare persuades us that here is a person free of the superego. The chronological sequence begins with my favorite essay on Falstaff, Harold Goddard's celebration of the fat knight's vision of "life for the fun of it."

Wyndham Lewis, English polemicist and totalitarian Modernist, more darkly sees a shamanistic Falstaff, an English *Machiavel,* "a hero run hugely to seed." A more balanced estimate is provided by C. L. Barber's study of "rule and misrule," in which Falstaff appears as a Lord of Misrule, whose eventual dismissal is both a dramatic and a social necessity though it is achieved at the high cost of blocking off an awareness of irony.

Ricardo J. Quinones, chronicling the "growth" of Prince Hal, sees him as a master of the demands of any particular time, while Falstaff rejects time. From another perspective, that of a more dialectical criticism, Michael McCanles judges the early attitudes of Falstaff and Hal, however diverse, to be dialectically correlative, for "when anyone in this play affects one side of a moral antinomy in conscious contradistinction to its opposite, he is doomed to enact both opposites, and not know it." Elliot Krieger, in a professedly Marxist reading, describes a Prince Hal who "enacts within the tavern his ambivalent relation to authority."

In an analysis of what he calls "Prince Hal's joke," David Sundelson shrewdly finds it to be one in which "Hal celebrates himself as multiple but whole and potent," a master of gestures that are "ambiguous and solipsistic." A. D. Nuttall, as part of his brilliant exegesis of Shakespearean mimesis, contrasts Hal, "a mode of goodness which is embarrassing," to

Falstaff, who "spans and sums in his person all change, all shocks," and who is "a Dido in the form of an Anchises."

The last word in this volume, happily, is given to E. Talbot Donaldson, our greatest Chaucerian, who speculates splendidly on the influence relationship between Chaucer's Wife of Bath and Falstaff, two of the most authentic heroic vitalists in all of literature.

Introduction

Falstaff is to the world of the histories what Shylock is to the comedies and
Hamlet to the tragedies: *the* problematical representation. Falstaff, Shylock,
Hamlet put to us the question: precisely how does Shakespearean representation differ from anything before it, and how has it overdetermined
our expectations of representation ever since?

The fortunes of Falstaff in scholarship and criticism have been endlessly
dismal, and I will not resume them here. I prefer Harold Goddard on Falstaff
to any other commentator, and yet I am aware that Goddard appears to
have sentimentalized and even idealized Falstaff. I would say better that
than the endless litany absurdly patronizing Falstaff as Vice, Parasite, Fool,
Braggart Soldier, Corrupt Glutton, Seducer of Youth, Cowardly Liar, and
everything else that would not earn the greatest wit in all literature an
honorary degree at Yale or a place on the board of the Ford Foundation.

Falstaff, I will venture, in Shakespeare rather than in Verdi, is precisely
what Nietzsche tragically attempted yet failed to represent in his Zarathustra: a person without a superego, or should I say, Socrates without the
daimon. Perhaps even better, Falstaff is not the Sancho Panza of Cervantes,
but the exemplary figure of Kafka's parable "The Truth about Sancho
Panza." Kafka's Sancho Panza, a free man, has diverted his *daimon* from
him by many nightly feedings of chivalric romances (it would be science
fiction nowadays). Diverted from Sancho, his true object, the *daimon* becomes the harmless Don Quixote, whose mishaps prove edifying enter-
tainment for the "philosophic" Sancho, who proceeds to follow his errant
daimon, out of a sense of responsibility. Falstaff's "failure," if it can be
termed that, is that he fell in love, not with his own *daimon*, but with his
bad son, Hal, who all too truly is Bolingbroke's son. The witty knight
should have diverted his own *daimon* with Shakespearean comedies, and
philosophically have followed the *daimon* off to the forest of Arden.

Falstaff is neither good enough nor bad enough to flourish in the world of the histories. But then he is necessarily beyond, not only good and evil, but cause and effect as well. A greater monist than the young Milton, Falstaff plays at dualism partly in order to mock all dualisms, whether Christian, Platonic, or even the Freudian dualism that he both anticipates and in some sense refutes.

Falstaff provoked the best of all critics, Dr. Johnson, into the judgment that "he has nothing in him that can be esteemed." George Bernard Shaw, perhaps out of envy, called Falstaff "a besotted and disgusting old wretch." Yet Falstaff's sole rival in Shakespeare is Hamlet; no one else, as Oscar Wilde noted, has so comprehensive a consciousness. Representation itself changed permanently because of Hamlet and Falstaff. I begin with my personal favorite among all of Falstaff's remarks, if only because I plagiarize it daily:

> O, thou has damnable iteration, and art indeed able to corrupt a saint. Thou hast done much harm upon me, Hal, God forgive thee for it! Before I knew thee, Hal, I knew nothing, and now am I, if a man should speak truly, little better than one of the wicked.

W. H. Auden, whose Falstaff essentially was Verdi's, believed the knight to be "a comic symbol for the supernatural order of charity" and thus a displacement of Christ into the world of wit. The charm of this reading, though considerable, neglects Falstaff's grandest quality, his immanence. He is as immanent a representation as Hamlet is transcendent. Better than any formulation of Freud's, Falstaff perpetually shows us that the ego indeed is always a bodily ego. And the bodily ego is always vulnerable, and Hal indeed has done much harm upon it, and will do far worse, and will need forgiveness, though no sensitive audience ever will forgive him. Falstaff, like Hamlet, and like Lear's Fool, does speak truly, and Falstaff remains, despite Hal, rather better than one of the wicked, or the good.

For what is supreme immanence in what might be called the order of representation? This is another way of asking: is not Falstaff, like Hamlet, so original a representation that he originates much of what we know or expect about representation? We cannot see how original Falstaff is because Falstaff *contains* us; we do not contain him. And though we love Falstaff, he does not need our love any more than Hamlet does. His sorrow is that he loves Hal rather more than Hamlet loves Ophelia, or even Gertrude. The Hamlet of act 5 is past loving anyone, but that is a gift (if it is a gift) resulting from transcendence. If you dwell wholly in this world, and if you are, as Falstaff is, a *pervasive* entity, or as Freud would say, "a strong egoism," then you must begin to love, as Freud also says, in order that you may not fall ill. But what if your strong egoism is not afflicted by any ego-ideal, what if you are never watched, or watched over, by what is above the ego? Falstaff is *not* subject to a power that watches, discovers and criticizes all his intentions. Falstaff, except for his single and misplaced love, is free, is freedom itself, because he seems free of the superego.

II

Why does Falstaff (and not his parody in *The Merry Wives of Windsor*) pervade histories rather than comedies? To begin is to be free, and you cannot begin freshly in comedy any more than you can in tragedy. Both genres are family romances, at least in Shakespeare. History in Shakespeare is hardly the genre of freedom for kings and nobles, but it is for Falstaff. How and why? Falstaff is of course his own mother and his own father, begotten out of wit by caprice. Ideally he wants nothing except the audience, which he always has; who could watch anyone else on stage when Ralph Richardson was playing Falstaff? Not so ideally, he evidently wants the love of a son, and invests in Hal, the impossible object. But primarily he has what he must have, the audience's fascination with the ultimate image of freedom. His precursor in Shakespeare is not Puck or Bottom, but Faulconbridge the Bastard in *The Life and Death of King John*. Each has a way of providing a daemonic chorus that renders silly all royal and noble squabbles and intrigues. The Bastard in *John*, forthright like his father Richard the Lion Heart, is not a wicked wit, but his truthtelling brutally prophesies Falstaff's function.

There are very nearly as many Falstaffs as there are critics, which probably is as it should be. These proliferating Falstaffs tend either to be degraded or idealized, again perhaps inevitably. One of the most ambiguous Falstaffs was created by the late Sir William Empson: "He is the scandalous upper-class man whose behavior embarrasses his class and thereby pleases the lower class in the audience, as an 'exposure.'" To Empson, Falstaff also was both nationalist and Machiavel, "and he had a dangerous amount of power." Empson shared the hint of Wyndham Lewis that Falstaff was homosexual, and so presumably lusted (doubtless in vain) after Hal. To complete this portrait, Empson added that Falstaff, being both an aristocrat and a mob leader, was "a familiar dangerous type," a sort of Alcibiades one presumes.

Confronted by so ambiguous a Falstaff, I return to the sublime knight's rhetoric, which I read very differently, since Falstaff's power seems to me not at all a matter of class, sexuality, politics, or nationalism. Power it is: sublime pathos, *potentia*, the drive for life, more life, at every and any cost. I will propose that Falstaff is neither a noble synecdoche nor a grand hyperbole, but rather a metalepsis or far-fetcher, to use Puttenham's term. To exist without a super ego is to be a solar trajectory, an ever-early brightness, which Nietzsche's Zarathustra, in his bathos, failed to be. "Try to live as though it were morning," Nietzsche advises. Falstaff does not need the advice, as we discover when we first encounter him:

> FALSTAFF: Now, Hal, what time of day is it, lad?
> PRINCE: Thou art so fat-witted with drinking of old sack, and
> unbuttoning thee after supper, and sleeping upon benches
> after noon, that thou hast forgotten to demand that truly
> which thou wouldest truly know. What a devil hast thou
> to do with the time of the day? unless hours were cups of
> sack, and minutes capons, and clocks the tongues of
> bawds, and dials the signs of leaping-houses, and the
> blessed sun himself a fair hot wench in flame-color'd
> taffata, I see no reason why thou shouldst be so
> superfluous to demand the time of the day.

I take it that wit here remains with Falstaff, who is not only witty in himself but the cause of wit in his ephebe, Prince Hal, who mocks his teacher, but in the teacher's own exuberant manner and mode. Perhaps there is a double meaning when Falstaff opens his reply with: "Indeed, you come near me now, Hal," since near is as close as the Prince is capable of, when he imitates the master. Master of what? is the crucial question, generally answered so badly. To take up the stance of most Shakespeare scholars is to associate Falstaff with "such inordinate and low desires, /Such poor, such bare, such lewd, such mean attempts,/ Such barren pleasures, rude society." I quote King Henry the Fourth, aggrieved usurper, whose description of Falstaff's aura is hardly recognizable to the audience. We recognize rather: "Counterfeit? I lie, I am no counterfeit. To die is to be a counterfeit, for he is but the counterfeit of a man who hath not the life of a man; but to counterfeit dying, when a man thereby liveth, is to be no counterfeit, but the true and perfect image of life indeed." As Falstaff rightly says, he has saved his life by counterfeiting death, and presumably the moralizing critics would be delighted had the unrespectable knight been butchered by Douglas, "that hot termagant Scot."

The true and perfect image of life, Falstaff, confirms his truth and perfection by counterfeiting dying and so evading death. Though he is given to parodying Puritan preachers, Falstaff has an authentic obsession with the dreadful parable of the rich man and Lazarus in Luke 16:19 ff. A certain rich man, a purple-clad glutton, is contrasted with the beggar Lazarus, who desired "to be fed with the crumbs which fell from the rich man's table: moreover the dogs came and licked his sores." Both glutton and beggar die, but Lazarus is carried into Abraham's bosom, and the purple glutton into hell, from which he cries vainly for Lazarus to come and cool his tongue. Falstaff stares at Bardolph, his Knight of the Burning Lamp, and affirms: "I never see thy face but I think upon hell-fire and Dives that liv'd in purple; for there he is in his robes, burning, burning." Confronting his hundred and fifty tattered prodigals, as he marches them off to be food for powder, Falstaff calls them "slaves as ragged as Lazarus in the painted cloth, where the glutton's dogs lick'd his sores." In *Henry IV, Part 2,* Falstaff's first speech again returns to this fearful text, as he cries out against one who denies him credit: "Let him be damn'd like the glutton! Pray God his tongue be hotter!" Despite the ironies abounding in Falstaff the glutton invoking Dives, Shakespeare reverses the New Testament, and Falstaff ends, like Lazarus, in Abraham's bosom, according to the convincing testimony of Mistress Quickly in *Henry V,* where Arthur Britishly replaces Abraham:

> BARDOLPH: Would I were with him, wheresome'er he is, either
> in heaven or in hell!
> HOSTESS: Nay sure, he's not in hell; he's in Arthur's bosom, if
> ever man went to Arthur's bosom. 'A made a finer end,
> and went away and it had been any christom child.

In dying, Falstaff is a newly baptized child, innocent of all stain. The pattern of allusions to Luke suggests a crossing over, with the rejected Falstaff a poor Lazarus upon his knees in front of Dives wearing the royal purple of Henry V. To a moralizing critic this is outrageous, but Shakespeare does stranger tricks with biblical texts. Juxtapose the two moments:

> FALSTAFF: My King, my Jove! I speak to thee, my heart!
> KING: I know thee not, old man, fall to thy prayers.
> How ill white hairs becomes a fool and jester!
> I have long dreamt of such a kind of man,
> So surfeit-swell'd, so old, and so profane;
> But being awak'd, I do despise my dream.

And here is Abraham, refusing to let Lazarus come to comfort the "clothed in purple" Dives:

> And beside all this, between us and you there is a great gulf
> fixed: so that they which would pass from hence to you cannot;
> neither can they pass to us, that would come from thence.

Wherever Henry V is, he is not in Arthur's bosom, with the rejected Falstaff.

III

I suggest that Shakespearean representation in the histories indeed demands our understanding of what Shakespeare did to history, in contrast to what his contemporaries did. Standard scholarly views of literary history, and all Marxist reductions of literature and history alike, have the curious allied trait of working very well for, say, Thomas Dekker, but being absurdly irrelevant for Shakespeare. Falstaff and the Tudor theory of kingship? Falstaff and surplus value? I would prefer Falstaff and Nietzsche's vision of the use and abuse of history for life, if it were not that Falstaff triumphs precisely where the Overman fails. One can read Freud on our discomfort in culture backwards, and get somewhere close to Falstaff, but the problem again is that Falstaff triumphs precisely where Freud denies that triumph is possible. With Falstaff as with Hamlet (and, perhaps, with Cleopatra) Shakespearean representation is so self-begotten and so influential that we can apprehend it only by seeing that it originates us. We cannot judge a mode of representation that has overdetermined our ideas of representation. Like only a few other authors—the Yahwist, Chaucer, Cervantes, Tolstoy—Shakespeare calls recent critiques of literary representation severely into doubt. Jacob, the Pardoner, Sancho Panza, Hadji Murad: it seems absurd to call them figures of rhetoric, let alone to see Falstaff, Hamlet, Shylock, Cleopatra as tropes of ethos and/or of pathos. Falstaff is not language but diction, the product of Shakespeare's will over language, a will that changes characters through and by what they say. Most simply, Falstaff is not how meaning is renewed, but rather how meaning gets started.

Falstaff is so profoundly original a representation because most truly he represents the essence of invention, which is the essence of poetry. He is a perpetual catastrophe, a continuous transference, a universal family romance. If Hamlet is beyond us and beyond our need of him, so that we require our introjection of Horatio, so as to identify ourselves with Horatio's love for Hamlet, then Falstaff too is beyond us. But in the Falstaffian beyonding, as it were, in what I think we must call the Falstaffian sublimity, we are never permitted by Shakespeare to identify ourselves with the Prince's ambivalent affection for Falstaff. Future monarchs have no friends, only followers, and Falstaff, the man without a superego, is no one's follower. Freud never speculated as to what a person without a superego would be like, perhaps because that had been the dangerous prophecy of Nietzsche's Zarathustra. Is there not some sense in which Falstaff's whole being implicitly says to us: "The wisest among you is also merely a conflict and a hybrid between plant and phantom. But do I bid you become phantoms or plants?" Historical critics who call Falstaff a phantom, and moral critics who judge Falstaff to be a plant, can be left to be answered by Sir John himself. Even in his debased form, in *The Merry Wives of Windsor*, he crushes them thus:

> Have I liv'd to stand at the taunt of one that makes fritters of English? This is enough to be the decay of lust and late-walking through the realm.

But most of all Falstaff is a reproach to all critics who seek to demystify mimesis, whether by Marxist or deconstructionist dialectics. Like Hamlet, Falstaff is a super-mimesis, and so compels us to see aspects of reality we otherwise could never apprehend. Marx would teach us what he calls "the appropriation of human reality" and so the appropriation also of human suffering. Nietzsche and his deconstructionist descendants would teach us the necessary irony of failure in every attempt to represent human reality. Falstaff, being more of an original, teaches us himself: "No, that's certain, I am not a double man; but if I be not Jack Falstaff, then am I a Jack." A double man is either a phantom or two men, and a man who is two men might as well be a plant. Sir John is Jack Falstaff; it is the Prince who is a Jack or rascal, and so are Falstaff's moralizing critics. We are in no position then to judge Falstaff or to assess him as a representation of reality. Hamlet is too dispassionate even to *want* to contain us. Falstaff is passionate and challenges us not to bore him, if he is to deign to represent us.

Henry IV

Harold C. Goddard

The two parts of *King Henry IV* are really a single drama in ten acts. Indeed the best things in *Part 3* are invisible when it stands by itself, more proof, if any were needed, that Shakespeare did not think in purely theatrical terms, for staging the two parts as one play must always have been impracticable, and the second part has seldom been produced in our day.

The richness and complexity of this double drama may be seen in the fact that any one of three men may with reason be regarded as its central figure. If we think of it as a continuation of the story of Henry Bolingbroke who deposed and murdered Richard II, then King Henry IV, as the title implies, is the protagonist. If we conceive it as background and preface to Henry V, Prince Hal is central. But if we just give ourselves to it spontaneously as the spectator or naïve reader does, the chances are that the comic element will overbalance the historical. Sir John runs away with us as some critics think he did with the author. In that case these are "the Falstaff plays," and Falstaff himself the most important as he certainly is the most captivating figure in them. By stretching a point we might even find a fourth "hero": there have been productions of *Part 1* in which Hotspur has outshone the other three. But that must have been a chance of casting, or miscasting.

II

In *Richard II* Shakespeare interred the doctrine of the divine right of kings. In *Henry IV* he tries out what can be said for the opposing theory.

From *The Meaning of Shakespeare.* © 1951 by the University of Chicago. The University of Chicago Press, 1951.

The twentieth century has fought two wars at enormous cost of life and treasure to avert the threat of the "strong" man. It is a pity that it could not have paid more attention in advance to Shakespeare's analysis and annihilation of this type and theory in his History Plays, particularly to the story of King Henry IV. Richard III was a "strong man" melodramatically represented. Pandulph, arch-power-politician of *King John*, was another, done closer to life. But compared with Henry IV either of these was a stage Machiavel with the label "Villain" on his sleeve. Henry, whatever he became, was natively neither cruel nor tyrannical, but a man of intelligence and insight and not devoid of a sense of justice. His story for that reason approximates tragedy.

The hypocrite has always been a favorite subject of satire. Henry IV is one of the most subtly drawn and effective hypocrites in literature, in no small measure because the author keeps his portrayal free of any satirical note. But not of any ironical note. Richard II had done Henry an injustice in banishing him and confiscating his inheritance. Coming back, the exile discovers that the opportunity to right his personal wrongs coincides with the chance to rid his native land of a weak king. So he finds himself ascending the throne almost before he knows it. Or so at least he protests later.

> Though then, God knows, I had no such intent,
> But that necessity so bow'd the state
> That I and greatness were compell'd to kiss.

"Necessity, the tyrant's plea." As previously in *The Rape of Lucrece*, as later in *Macbeth*, as so often in all literature from Aeschylus to Dostoevsky, opportunity is here made the mother of crime. And the punishment, though delayed outwardly, inwardly is immediate. It comes in the form of fear. Confirming a change that had long been in incubation, on the day when Henry deposed Richard he became a double man, one thing to the world, another to his own conscience. Force gives birth to fear. Fear gives birth to lies. And fear and lies together give birth to more force. Richard, symbol of Henry's own unjust act, had to be put out of the way. From the moment Henry gave the hint that ended in Richard's death to the moment of his own death at the end of *2 Henry IV*, his life became a continuous embodiment of the strange law whereby we come to resemble what we fear. The basis of that law is plain. What we are afraid of we keep in mind. What we keep in mind we grow like unto.

Already at the conclusion of the play that bears Richard's name that nemesis had begun to work. Near its beginning Richard banished two men, Henry and Mowbray, who were symbols of his own fear and guilt. He wanted them out of his sight. At the end of the same play Henry does the same thing. He banishes Carlisle and Exton. He wants them out of his sight—Carlisle because he is a symbol of truth and loyalty to Richard, Exton because he has been his instrument in Richard's murder.

Shakespeare dramatizes these ideas with impressive brevity and power. Unknown to Henry, the coffin containing Richard's body is at the door. It is as if the victim's ghost rises then and there from the dead and as if Henry, sensing its nearness, spares Carlisle's life in hope of indulgence. But to grant the Bishop a full pardon is beyond his power, for he could not endure the perpetual accusation and conviction of his presence. So he tells him to

> Choose out some secret place, some reverend room,

in which to spend the rest of his life. (It is like a prophecy of the Jerusalem Chamber in which Henry's own life was to end.) At that moment Exton enters, "with attendants bearing a coffin," and announces:

> Great king, within this coffin I present
> Thy buried fear.

By "buried fear" Exton of course means "the body of the man you feared." But the future reads into those three words another and more fearful meaning. It was indeed a buried fear, a fear buried deep in Henry's breast, that that coffin contained, a fear that was to shape every act and almost every thought of that "great king" henceforth. The spirit of the man who had once banished him and whom he had deposed enters his body and deposes and banishes his own spirit. When Henry bids Exton

> With Cain go wander through the shades of night,

it is to his own soul that, unawares, he issues that order. The later soliloquy on sleep shows through what shades of night that soul was destined to wander. From the moment he mentions the name of Cain, Henry's story is the story of the buried Richard within him:

> Lords, I protest, my soul is full of woe,
> That blood should sprinkle me to make me grow.

We do not need to wait for *Hamlet* to know that Henry "doth protest too much." It is not a protest but a confession. And to compensate for his crime in the eyes of the world, he decrees

> a voyage to the Holy Land,
> To wash this blood off from my guilty hand.

III

1 Henry IV opens with a proclamation of peace and a definite proposal of the promised crusade to the sepulcher of Christ:

> To chase these pagans in those holy fields
> Over whose acres walk'd those blessed feet
> Which fourteen hundred years ago were nail'd
> For our advantage on the bitter cross.

It must have seemed to the pagans on odd way of instituting peace. But pagans of course did not count as human beings to Henry. There sounds, however, a note of something like genuine contrition in the reference to Christ. Yet, on his deathbed, Henry was to confess explicitly that this crusade was a purely political move to distract attention from civil unrest!

For the usual thing had happened. The men who helped Henry to the throne (the Percys) grew envious of the power they did not share and of his friendship:

> The king will always think him in our debt,
> And think we think ourselves unsatisfied,
> Till he hath found a time to pay us home.

This suspicion, reciprocated, led to acts on both sides that put foundations under it with the result that Henry's reign, where it was not open war, was incessant dissension.

Henry has no sooner declared the end of "civil butchery" in the opening speech of the play than a messenger from Wales enters announcing a thousand men "butcher'd" by the wild and irregular Glendower. And on the heels of this, news from Scotland: Hotspur has met and defeated the Scots. Ten thousand of them slain, and prisoners taken. But their captor refuses to hand them over to the king! This must be looked into. The pilgrimage to Jerusalem must be postponed.

A bit later the king confronts the Percys: father, son, and uncle. He declares that he has been too forbearing in the past, "smooth as oil, soft as young down," and implies that from now on he will demand the respect due him. Worcester bids him remember who helped him to his throne. To which the king retorts:

> Worcester, get thee gone; for I do see
> Danger and disobedience in thine eye.

The ghost of Richard again! Henry solving a problem by pushing it out of sight, doing to his enemy exactly what Richard did to him! The "buried fear" is stirring in its grave.

And the king's self-control is in for an even more severe jolt. Hotspur refuses to give up his prisoners unless his brother-in-law, Mortimer, who has been captured by the Welshman Glendower, shall be ransomed. At the mention of Mortimer something seems to explode inside the king:

> Let me not hear you speak of Mortimer;
> Send me your prisoners with the speediest means
> Or you shall hear in such a kind from me
> As will displease you.

Can this be Henry? The tone, so unlike him, shows that the name of Mortimer has touched something at the very foundation of his nature. When the king, in high dudgeon, has gone out, Worcester explains. Mortimer is legal heir to the throne: so by right, and so proclaimed by Richard. Of what avail to have had Richard murdered if his title transmigrated into a living man?

This is news to Hotspur. Mortimer! With the diabolic insight of a small boy who has hit on a scheme for teasing his sister, he dances about in an ecstasy and cries:

> I will find him when he lies asleep,
> And in his ear I'll holla "Mortimer!"
> Nay,
> I'll have a starling shall be taught to speak
> Nothing but "Mortimer," and give it him,
> To keep his anger still in motion.

Henry stands revealed to him for the hypocrite he is: a "vile politician," a "fawning greyhound," a "king of smiles."

Forthwith the three Percys hatch a plot to unite under themselves the Scots, the Welsh, and the Archbishop of York and, with Mortimer as the cutting edge, to defy the king. I said that three men, or even four, contend for the primacy in this play. And now we have a fifth. Mortimer is on the stage in only one scene. But he is the play's mainspring as certainly as is the Ghost in *Hamlet*. Shakespeare grew more and more fond of quietly suggesting the immense dramatic importance of figures partly or wholly behind the action, of making the absent present. (Shakespeare may have gotten the hint for this technique from the painting. Note this stanza from the description of the picture of the Siege of Troy in *The Rape of Lucrece*:

"For much imaginary work was there;
Conceit deceitful, so compact, so kind,
That for Achilles' image stood his spear
Gripp'd in an armed hand; himself, behind,
Was left unseen, save to the eye of mind:
   A hand, a foot, a face, a leg, a head,
   Stood for the whole to be imagined.'')

IV

These Percys, who having made a king now plan to unmake him, are an interesting group. They take up, both singly and together, the theme that Richard II introduced and Henry IV continued, and play their variations on it, the theme of fear and lies—and the violence to which they inevitably give rise. Shakespeare seems as bent on getting together every known type of duplicity, counterfeit, and deceit in this play as a boy is on collecting every kind of bird's egg.

The elder Henry, Earl of Northumberland, the main factor in Bolingbroke's elevation to the throne, is remembered as the man who in the abdication scene kicked Richard when he was down. Confirming the old proverb about the bully, he is the archcoward of *Henry IV*. He ruins the cause of the rebellion against the king by his fears, his delays, his faking of illness, his running away. While his son is fighting and dying at Shrewsbury, he lies "crafty-sick" in his castle. When his party rallies after its defeat, he starts north for Scotland.

Thomas Percy, Henry's brother, Earl of Worcester, is hardly more attractive. He is a sour, dour, suspicious, and jealous man, envious himself and therefore counting on and helping to create envy in Henry. His concealment from Hotspur of the king's offer of peace before the battle of Shrewsbury is characteristic of him. If his brother is the coward, he is the liar.

And finally there is the younger Henry, "the Hotspur of the North; he that kills me some six or seven dozen of Scots at a breakfast, washes his hands, and says to his wife, 'Fie upon this quiet life! I want work.' " The colorful Hotspur at any rate, it will be said, is in another world from his father and uncle. In one sense he is indeed their utter antithesis. But in another he is more like them than he seems. One cannot help loving Hotspur for his blunt honesty. It seems almost his central quality. And yet his very honesty is based on a lie, a degenerate form of the medieval conception of "honour." The fact that Hotspur talks so incessantly and extravagantly about "honour" shows that he distrusts his own faith in it. He is another who "doth protest too much." This fact is clinched by his uneasy sleep, which his wife reveals. He fights all night long in his dreams. We are reminded of Richard III's "timorous dreams," which *his* wife reveals. Far as the noble Hotspur is from the villainous Richard, the psychology is the same. It is fear begotten by falsehood.

The undegenerate chivalric conception of honor was a lofty one. Under it trial by battle, and war, became religious affairs. Courage and morale were given a religious ground. God was in the right arm of the man whose cause was righteous, and to win under his sanction was to cover oneself with glory, the glory of God himself. But the line between war for God's sake and war for war's sake can become a very thin one to one who enjoys fighting. It does in Hotspur's case. He rationalizes his unborn pugnacity into a creed. War to him is the natural state of man, the noble as well as the royal occupation. It is what art for art's sake is to the artist. He is the extreme antitype of that "certain lord," that "popinjay," who, fresh as a bridegroom, accosted him, when he was breathless and faint from fighting, with the declaration

> that it was a great pity, so it was,
> This villanous saltpetre should be digg'd
> Out of the bowels of the harmless earth,
> Which many a good tall fellow had destroy'd
> So cowardly; and but for these vile guns,
> He would himself have been a soldier.

Militarism and pacifism have always had a strange family resemblance, and Hotspur and his popinjay are equally deluded. To put Hotspur beside that other picturesque talker and valiant fighter, Faulconbridge, is to put the "idealism" of war beside its realism, to the immense disadvantage of the former.

But we must be fair to Hotspur. There are plenty of echoes in him of the great tradition from which he comes. When he hears that his father has failed them on the eve of battle, and cries,

> It lends a lustre and more great opinion,
> A larger dare to our great enterprise,

he anticipates the Winston Churchill of 1940. Even finer is his

> the time of life is short;
> To spend that shortness basely were too long.

And when he bids them on the field of Shrewsbury

> Sound all the lofty instruments of war,
> And by that music let us all embrace,

it is as intoxicating as fife and drum to a small boy. But that is the trouble. Hotspur intoxicates himself with "honour," and when "the morning after" comes he is capable of saying, for example, that he would have Prince Hal poisoned with a pot of ale if he weren't afraid that it would please the king, his father. When honor has come to that pass, it is ready to be debunked. Falstaff is on the horizon. When the play is done, there is about as much left of "honour" as there was of the divine right of kings at the end of *Richard II*. In fact the sentimental Richard and the pugnacious Hotspur are closer to each other than they look. They are both victims of words.

V

And this brings us to the fourth and last of the Henrys in what are sometimes appropriately called these "Henry" plays: Henry, Prince of Wales, *alias* Harry, *alias* Hal, companion of Falstaff and heir apparent to the throne. His father first introduces us to him in the last act of *Richard II* when he asks,

> Can no man tell me of my unthrifty son?

and goes on to confess the low resorts that he haunts with a crew of dissolute companions, even the robberies he commits in their company. So at least the reports have it that have come to him. And Hotspur, who has recently talked with the Prince, more than confirms them. He tells specifically of Hal's intention to burlesque the spirit of chivalry in the spirit of the brothel.

With this glimpse of the heir to the throne added to what we have seen of the other three Henrys, the political pattern of these plays becomes clear. Henry IV, by deposing his legitimate sovereign, Richard, has committed himself to the best-man theory of kingship, which, in practice, is equivalent to the strong-man theory. Between himself and Richard, in his own opinion and in that of many others, there could be no question of relative merit. But here is Hotspur, the incarnation of valor (and brother-in-law incidentally of Mortimer, legal heir to the throne). And here is his own good-for-nothing son. What about the succession in this case, on the King's own theory?

Plainly Henry's revised version of the divine right of kings is in for trouble. He is caught in his own trap. And the nemesis is personal as well as political. "What the father hath hid cometh out in the son," says Nietzsche, "and often have I found the son a father's revealed secret." There was never a better illustration of this truth. In his concentration on power the elder Henry has suppressed both the playful and the passionate tendencies of his nature.

> My blood hath been too cold and temperate.

What he has kept under comes out in Hal, who leads a life of abandon under the tutelage of Falstaff. We are told little of the early life of the king. But what he says of his son is sufficient:

> Most subject is the fattest soil to weeds;
> And he, the noble image of my youth,
> Is overspread with them: therefore my grief
> Stretches beyond the hour of death.

Evidently Henry had had his fling too. His "grief" is partly unconscious envy—regret for his own lost youth, like that of that other hypocrite, Polonius, when he sent his son to Paris. But the important point is that the king recognizes his earlier self in his son.

Though it comes later, it is Henry's great soliloquy on sleep that confirms all this.

> "How many thousand of my poorest subjects
> Are at this hour asleep! O sleep, O gentle sleep,
> Nature's soft nurse, how have I frighted thee
> That thou no more wilt weigh my eyelids down
> And steep my senses in forgetfulness?
> Why rather, sleep, liest thou in smoky cribs,
> Upon uneasy pallets stretching thee,
> And hush'd with buzzing night-flies to thy slumber,
> Than in the perfum'd chambers of the great
> Under the canopies of costly state,
> And lull'd with the sound of sweetest melody?
> O thou dull god, why liest thou with the vile
> In loathsome beds, and leav'st the kingly couch
> A watch-case or a common 'larum-bell?
> Wilt thou upon the high and giddy mast
> Seal up the ship-boy's eyes, and rock his brains
> In cradle of the rude imperious surge
> And in the visitation of the winds,
> Who take the ruffian billows by the top,
> Curling their monstrous heads and hanging them

> With deaf'ning clamour in the slippery clouds,
> That, with the hurly, death itself awakes?
> Canst thou, O partial sleep, give thy repose
> To the wet sea-boy in an hour so rude,
> And in the calmest and most stillest night,
> With all appliances and means to boot,
> Deny it to a king? Then happy low, lie down!
> Uneasy lies the head that wears a crown."

It is the nocturnal part of a man that receives what he puts behind his back or under his feet in the daytime. In the apostrophe to sleep this victim of insomnia reveals the unrealized half of his soul. The lines have been called out of character. They are Shakespeare the poet, we are told, running away with Shakespeare the dramatist; Henry was incapable of anything so imaginative. On the contrary, the soliloquy is a measure of the amount of imagination that must be repressed before nature will permit one of her own creatures to be transformed into a worldling. It defines the distance Henry has travelled from innocence, and, in contrast with his diurnal aspect, the thickness of the mask that rank imposes.

> The king hath many marching in his coats,

cries Hotspur at Shrewsbury, referring to the counterfeit "kings" sent into the battle line in royal costume to lessen the chances of the real king's death. The device is a symbol of the man—as he became. The soliloquy on sleep tells us what he might have become.

When it is a question of the prince, his father is honest and intelligent enough to perceive that he is himself trying to eat his cake and have it. The doctrine of the strong man and the doctrine of hereditary succession, he sees, do not cohere when the son is unworthy of the father. He catches the deadly parallel between the unkingly Richard and his own unkingly son and puts it in so many words to Hal:

> For all the world
> As thou art to this hour was Richard then
> When I from France set foot at Ravenspurgh,
> And even as I was then is Percy now.
> Now, by my sceptre and my soul to boot,
> He hath more worthy interest to the state
> Than thou the shadow of succession.

As Henry was to Richard, so is Hotspur now to Hal. There it is in a sentence. Hal gets the point and promises to be more himself in the future—

at Hotspur's expense. The latter has been busy storing up glorious deeds all his life. Now Hal will make him exchange those deeds for his own "indignities."

> This, in the name of God, I promise here . . .
> And I will die a hundred thousand deaths
> Ere break the smallest parcel of this vow.

To which boast his delighted father replies:

> A hundred thousand rebels die in this.

The Prodigal Son has returned and the father has forgiven him! So at any rate it seems to those who make this play a fresh version of the biblical story. It is temptingly simple. But it leaves several things out of account.

To begin with, long before the prince made to his father the promise to reform, he made it to himself. Left alone at the end of the scene in which we first see him, he breaks out into the memorable words which, though they have been quoted so often, must be quoted once more:

> I know you all, and will awhile uphold
> The unyok'd humour of your idleness:
> Yet herein will I imitate the sun,
> Who doth permit the base contagious clouds
> To smother up his beauty from the world,
> That, when he please again to be himself,
> Being wanted, he may be more wonder'd at,
> By breaking through the foul and ugly mists
> Of vapours that did seem to strangle him.
> If all the year were playing holidays,
> To sport would be as tedious as to work;
> But when they seldom come, they wish'd for come,
> And nothing pleaseth but rare accidents.
> So, when this loose behaviour I throw off
> And pay the debt I never promised,
> By how much better than my word I am,
> By so much shall I falsify men's hopes;
> And like bright metal on a sullen ground,
> My reformation, glittering o'er my fault,
> Shall show more goodly and attract more eyes
> Than that which hath no foil to set it off.
> I'll so offend, to make offence a skill;
> Redeeming time when men think least I will.

On top of our first glimpse of the carefree Hal, these lines come with a painful shock, casting both backward and forward, as they do, a shadow of insincerity. At a first reading or witnessing of the play the soliloquy is soon forgotten. But when we return to the text, there it is! So all this unaffected fun was not unaffected after all. Affected, according to Hal, is precisely what it was, put on for a purpose—only perhaps, deep down, it was just the other way around, perhaps it was the fun that was unaffected and it was the desire to make a dramatic impression on the world that was put on.

The speech just doesn't cohere with the Hal we love, his admirers protest. It is out of character. It is Shakespeare speaking, not Henry. And in support of them, the historical critics point out that the poet was merely following a familiar Elizabethan convention of tipping off the audience that they might be in the secret. It is odd, however, if it is just Shakespeare, that he made the speech so long and detailed and chose to base it on a metaphor that was forever running through Henry's mind. The playwright could have given the necessary information in a quarter of the space.

It is true that the soliloquy is unlike Hal. Yet there is not a speech in the role more strictly in character. How can that be? It can be for the simple reason that it is not Hal, primarily, who makes the speech at all. The prince makes it. There are two Henrys. This is no quibble; it is the inmost heart of the matter. We saw that there were two elder Henrys. The king who had Richard murdered bears little resemblance to the man who utters the soliloquy on sleep. There are two younger Henrys who resemble each other just as little. If we need authority for what page after page of the play drives home, we have it in Falstaff, who makes just this distinction:

> PRINCE: Darest thou be as good as thy work now?
> FALSTAFF: Why, Hal, thou knowest, as thou art but man, I
> dare; but as thou art Prince, I fear thee as I fear the
> roaring of the lion's whelp.

Hal and the prince: we shall never get anything straight about this story if we confuse them or fail to mark the differences, the connections, and the interplay of the two. Talk about the Prodigal Son! There is indeed more than a touch of him in Hal; but in the deliberately and coldly ambitious prince not a spark. In him the Prodigal was reformed before he ever came into existence.

The Henry who is the prince is, appropriately, like the Henry who is the king, the son like the father. And Shakespeare takes the utmost pains to point this out. The theme of the famous soliloquy is the function of the foil. The prince says he will imitate the sun and suddenly appear from behind clouds at the theatrical moment to dazzle all beholders. Well, turn to that heart-to-heart talk between the king and his heir that ends in the latter's promise to amend his ways, and straight from the father's mouth we have the son's philosophy. The elder Henry tells how in earlier days he kept himself from the public gaze and dressed himself in humility in contrast with Richard, so that

> By being seldom seen, I could not stir
> But like a comet I was wonder'd at;
> That men would tell their children, "This is he";
> Others would say, "Where, which is Bolingbroke?"

Whereas Richard (and Hal of course catches the point)

> Grew a companion to the common streets . . .
> So when he had occasion to be seen,
> He was but as the cuckoo is in June,
> Heard, not regarded; seen, but with such eyes
> As, sick and blunted with community,
> Afford no extraordinary gaze,
> Such as is bent on sun–like majesty
> When it shines seldom in admiring eyes.

Not only the prince's idea. His very metaphor! The young man has already bettered his adviser in advance. His opening soliloquy was nothing but a variation on his father's theme: the uses of contrast. But the father kept himself rare, it will be said, while the son made himself common, acting like Richard instead of following his father's example. That was indeed the ground of the king's complaint. But he got the truth there exactly upside down. He did not see that his son was acting far more like himself than he was like Richard. The prince was doing precisely what his father had done, only in a wilier way. The king had kept himself literally hidden and then suddenly appeared. The prince was keeping himself figuratively hidden by his wild ways in order to emerge all at once as a self-disciplined king. As between the two, who can question which was the more dramatic and effective? But we like neither father nor son for his tricks, no matter how well contrived or brilliantly executed. The better the worse, in fact, in both cases. "A great act has no subordinate mean ones," says Thoreau. In view of the elder Henry's abortive attempt to disprove this truth, we wonder whether the younger Henry will have better success.

    Yet even after hearing his confession that his escapades are a political experiment in which his heart is not enlisted, we go on to the tavern scenes with unaffected delight. Hal seems to throw himself into them with a zest that gives the lie to the idea that he is holding anything back. Like ourselves, he seems to have forgotten his own words and plunges into the fun for its own sake quite in Falstaff's spirit. Not only does he appear to, he does— Hal does, that is. But the prince is there in the background and occasionally intrudes. Then Hal will return and only the alertest sense can detect the prince's presence. This is in accord with common experience. Who has not found himself so changed today from what he was yesterday that he could easily believe that other fellow was another man? He was. These vaunted modern discoveries about dual and multiple personalities are not discoveries at all. Shakespeare understood all about them in the concrete. I have quoted Falstaff. Let me quote a more recent and not less profound psychologist, Dostoevsky.

The second chapter of Dostoevsky's *The Devils* (wrongly called in English *The Possessed*) is entitled "Prince Harry." In it we are given an account of the youth of Nikolay Vsyevolodovitch Stavrogin. Utterly neglected by his father, Nikolay is initiated at his mother's request into the military life, just as some higher aspirations are being awakened in him by his tutor. Soon strange rumors come home. The young man has suddenly taken to riotous living. He is indulging in all sorts of outrageous conduct. His mother is naturally alarmed. But the tutor reassures her. It is only the first effervescence of a too richly endowed nature. The storm will subside. It is "like the youth of Prince Harry, who caroused with Falstaff, Poins, and Mrs. Quickly, as described by Shakespeare." The mother listens eagerly and asks the tutor to explain his theory. She even, in the words of the author, "took up Shakespeare herself and with great attention and read the immortal chronicle. But it did not comfort her, and indeed she did not find the resemblance very striking." Neither may we, though we do not have the excuse of mother love to blind us. The resemblance is there just the same: the same charm, the same neglect, the same plunge into dissipation, the same outrageous pranks, the same contact with military life, the same impossibility of reconciling what seem like two different men. "I had expected to see a dirty ragamuffin, sodden with drink and debauchery," says the narrator of Nikolay's story. "He was, on the contrary, the most elegant gentleman I had ever met." One anecdote in particular clinches the parallelism. Leaning down to whisper something to the Governor of the Province, Nikolay, on one occasion, suddenly takes his ear between his teeth. The exact, if exaggerated, counterpart of Hal's striking the Chief Justice.

Henry IV gives us an analysis of his son's temperament in advising Hal's brother how to handle him. It would fit Nikolay nearly as well.

> blunt not his love,
> Nor lose the good advantage of his grace
> By seeming cold or careless of his will;
> For he is gracious, if he be observ'd:
> He hath a tear for pity and a hand
> Open as day for melting charity;
> Yet notwithstanding, being incens'd, he's flint,
> As humorous as winter, and as sudden
> As flaws congealed in the spring of day.
> His temper, therefore, must be well observ'd:
> Chide him for faults, and do it reverently,
> When you perceive his blood inclin'd to mirth;
> But, being moody, give him line and scope,
> Till that his passions, like a whale on ground,
> Confound themselves with working.

What in Henry's case is deep variation in mood amounts in Nikolay's to a pathological split in personality. If Nikolay's place in the world had been more comparable with Henry's, their histories might have been more alike than they were. Even so, the violence and tragedy that came from this division within the soul of Stavrogin are a profounder comment than any criticism could be on the gradual fading of the carefree Hal and the slow emergence of the formidable victor of Agincourt. Dostoevsky understood Shakespeare better than did either the tutor or the mother in his novel. His chapter title "Prince Harry" was no mistake.

But now comes the most remarkable fact: Falstaff diagnoses Hal precisely as Dostoevsky does Stavrogin! "Dost thou hear, Hal?" he cries, just after the ominous "knocking from within" which proves to be the Sheriff. "Dost thou hear, Hal? never call a true piece of gold a counterfeit: thou art essentially mad without seeming so." "Mad" appears to be just about the last word to apply to the self-controlled and cold-blooded Henry. He certainly does not seem mad. But that is precisely what Falstaff says. "Oh, but Falstaff was only joking!" it will be objected. Of course he was; but it is the very genius of Falstaff to utter truth in jest. There is madness and madness.

The moment we follow Falstaff's lead and cease thinking of Henry as Henry and conceive him as Hal-and-the-prince we see how right Shakespeare was to build this play on an alternation of "tavern" scenes and political-military ones. Instead of being just chronicle play relieved by comedy (as historians of the drama are bound to see it), what we have is a genuine integration, both psychological and dramatic, the alternating character of the scenes corresponding to the two sides of a dual personality.

VI

And now we come to the third candidate for the role of "hero" in these plays.

Who at this late date can hope to say a fresh word about Falstaff? Long since, his admirers and detractors have drained language dry in their efforts to characterize him, to give expression to their fascination or detestation. Glutton, drunkard, coward, liar, lecher, boaster, cheat, thief, rogue, ruffian, villain are a few of the terms that have been used to describe a man whom others find the very incarnation of charm, one of the liberators of the human spirit, the greatest comic figure in the history of literature. "A besotted and disgusting old wretch," Bernard Shaw calls him. And isn't he—this man who held up unprotected travelers for pastime, betrayed innocence in the person of his page, cheated a trusting and hard-working hostess, borrowed a thousand pounds from an old friend with no intention of repaying it, abused his commission by taking cash in lieu of military service, and insinuated his way into the graces of the heir apparent with an eye to later favor. And yet after three centuries there the old sinner sits, more invulnerable and full of smiles than ever, his sagging paunch shaking like a jelly, dodging or receiving full on, unperturbed, the missiles his enemies hurl at him. Which is he? A colossus of sack, sensuality, and sweat—or a wit and humorist so great that he can be compared only with his creator, a figure, to use one of Shakespeare's own great phrases, livelier than life? One might think there were two Falstaffs.

The trouble with the "besotted and disgusting old wretch" theory is that Shakespeare has given us that old wretch exactly, and he is another man: the Falstaff of *The Merry Wives of Windsor*. The disparagers of Falstaff generally make him out a mixture, in varying proportions, of this other Falstaff, Sir Toby Belch, and Parolles, each of whom was an incalculably inferior person. But to assert that Falstaff is another man is not saying that he does not have many or even all of the vices of the "old wretch" for whom his defamers mistake him. Salt is not sodium, but that is not saying that sodium is not a component of salt. The truth is that there *are* two Falstaffs, just as there are two Henrys, the Immoral Falstaff and the Immortal

Falstaff, and the dissension about the man comes from a failure to recognize that fact. That the two could inhabit one body would not be believed if Shakespeare had not proved that they could. That may be the reason why he made it so huge.

Curiously, there is no more convincing testimony to this double nature of the man than that offered by those who are post persistent in pointing out his depravity. In the very process of committing the old sinner to perdition they reveal that they have been unable to resist his seductiveness. Professor Stoll, for instance, dedicates twenty-six sections of a long and learned essay to the annihilation of the Falstaff that his congenital lovers love. And then he begins his twenty-seventh and last section with the words: "And yet people like Falstaff"! And before his first paragraph is done, all his previous labor is obliterated as we find him asserting that Falstaff is "supremely poetic" (even his most ardent admirers would hardly venture that "supremely") and that "his is in many ways the most marvelous prose ever penned." (It is, but how did the old sot, we wonder, ever acquire it?) Before his next paragraph is over, Stoll has called Falstaff "the very spirit of comradeship," "the king of companions," and "the prince of good fellows." "We, too, after all, like Prince Hal and Mrs. Quickly," he goes on, "take to a man because of his charm, if it be big enough, not because of his virtue; and as for Falstaff, we are bewitched with the rogue's company." (A Falstaff idolater could scarcely ask for more than that.) "Under the spell of his presence and speech," Stoll concludes, we should forget, as she does, the wrong he has done Mrs. Quickly, "did we not stop to think."

"Stop to think"! One may determine the orbit of the moon, or make an atomic bomb, by stopping to think, but when since the beginning of time did man ever get at the secret of another by means of the intellect? It is all right to stop to think after we have taken a character to our hearts, but to do so before we have is fatal. Dr. Johnson stopped to think about Falstaff and as a result he decided that "he has nothing in him that can be esteemed." A child would be ashamed of such a judgment. But a child would never be guilty of it. "As for *Henry IV*," wrote one of the most imaginatively gifted young women I have ever known, "I love it. And I must have an utterly vulgar nature, for I simply adore Falstaff. He is perfectly delightful—not a fault in his nature, and the Prince is a DEVIL to reject him." That young woman evidently did not "stop to think." When she does, she will moderate that "not a fault in his nature," for that is the function of thinking—to hold our imagination within bounds and cut down its excrescences. Meanwhile, Falstaff has captured her, and she has captured Falstaff, for, as Blake said, enthusiastic admiration is the first principle of knowledge, and the last. Those who think about Falstaff before they fall in love with him may say some just things about him but they will never enter into his secret. "Would I were with him, wheresome'er he is, either in heaven or in hell!" Those words of poor Bardolph on hearing the account of Falstaff's death remain the highest tribute he ever did or ever could receive. In their stark sincerity they are worthy (irreverent as the suggestion will seem to some) to be put beside Dante's sublime incarnation of the same idea in the Paolo and Francesca incident in *The Inferno*, or even beside the words addressed to the thief who repented on the cross.

The scholars have attempted to explain Falstaff by tracing his origins. He has been found, variously, to have developed from the Devil of the miracle plays, the Vice of the morality plays, the boasting soldier of Plautine comedy, and so on. Now roots, up to a certain point, are interesting, but it takes the sun to make them grow and to illuminate the flower. And I think in this case we can find both roots and sun without going outside Shakespeare. If so, it is one of the most striking confirmations to be found of the embryological nature of his development.

If I were seeking the embryo of Falstaff in Shakespeare's imagination, I should consider the claims of Bottom—of Bottom and another character in *A Midsummer Night's Dream*. "What!" it will be said, "the dull realistic Bottom and the lively witty Falstaff? They are nearer opposites." But embryos, it must be remembered, seldom resemble what they are destined to develop into. Bottom, like the physical Falstaff at least, is compact of the heaviness, the materiality, the reality of earth; and the ass's head that Puck bestows on him is abundantly deserved, not only in special reference to his brains but in its general implication of animality. But instead of letting himself be humiliated by it, Bottom sings, and Titania, Queen of the Fairies, her eyes anointed by the magic flower, awakening, mistakes him for an angel, and taking him in her arms, lulls him to sleep. The obvious meaning of the incident of course is that love is blind. Look at the asinine thing an infatuated woman will fall in love with! But whoever stops there, though he may have gotten the fun, has missed the beauty. The moment when Bottom emerges from his dream, as we pointed out when discussing *A Midsummer Night's Dream*, is Shakespeare at one of his pinnacles. By a stroke of genius he turns a purely farcical incident into nothing less than a parable of the Awakening of Imagination within Gross Matter. It is the poet's way of saying that even within the head of this foolish plebeian weaver a divine light can be kindled. Bottom is conscious of transcendent things when he comes to himself. A creation has taken place within him. He struggles, in vain, to express it, and, in his very failure, succeeds:

God's my life! . . . I have had a most rare vision. I have had a dream, past the wit of man to say what dream it was. Man is but an ass, if he go about to expound this dream. Methought I was—there is no man can tell what. Methought I was,—and methought I had,—but man is but a patch'd fool, if he will offer to say what methought I had. The eye of man hath not heard, the ear of man hath not seen, man's hand is not able to taste, his tongue to conceive, nor his heart to report, what my dream was. I will get Peter Quince to write a ballad of this dream. It shall be called "Bottom's Dream," because it hath no bottom.

The dreamer may still be Bottom. But the dream itself is Puck. For one moment the two are one. Ass or Angel? Perhaps Titania was not so deluded after all.

Do not misunderstand me. I am not suggesting that Shakespeare ever consciously connected Puck and Bottom with Falstaff in his own mind. But having achieved this inconceivable integration of the two, how easily his genius would be tempted to repeat the miracle on a grander scale: to create a perfect mountain of flesh and show how the same wonder could occur within it, not momentarily, but, humanly speaking, perpetually. That at any rate is what Falstaff is: Imagination conquering matter, spirit subduing flesh. Bottom was a weaver—a weaver of threads. "I would I were a weaver," Falstaff once exclaimed. He was a weaver—a weaver of spells. Here, if ever, is the embryology of the imagination. "Man is but a patch'd fool, if he will offer to say. . . ." Who cannot catch the very accent of Falstaff in that?

> I'll put a girdle round about the earth
> In forty minutes.

It might have been said of Falstaff's wit. His Bottom-like body is continually being dragged down, but his Puck-like spirit can hide in a thimble or pass through a keyhole as nimble as any fairy's. What wonder that this contradictory being—as deminatured as a satyr or a mermaid—who is forever repeating within himself the original miracle of creation, has taken on the proportions of a mythological figure. He seems at times more like a god than a man. His very solidity is solar, his rotundity cosmic. To estimate the refining power we must know the grossness of what is to be refined. To be astounded by what lifts we must know the weight of what is to be lifted. Falstaff is levitation overcoming gravitation. At his wittiest and most aerial, he is Ariel tossing the terrestrial globe in the air as if it were a ball.

And yet—as we must never forget—he is also that fat old sinner fast asleep and snoring behind the arras. The sins, in fact, are the very things that make the miracle astonishing, as the chains and ropes do a Houdini's escape.

To grasp Falstaff thus *sub specie aeternitatis* we must see him, as Titania did Bottom, with our imagination, not with our senses. And that is why we shall never see Falstaff on the stage. On the stage there the monster of flesh stands—made, we know, mainly of pillows—with all his sheer material bulk and greasy beefiness, a palpable candidate for perdition. It takes rare acting to rescue him from being physically repulsive. And as for the miracle—it just refuses to happen in a theater. It would take a child to melt this too too solid flesh into spirit. It would take Falstaff himself to act Falstaff. But in a book! On the stage of our imagination! That is another matter. There the miracle can occur—and does for thousands of readers. Falstaff is a touchstone to tell whether the juice of the magic flower has been squeezed into our eyes. If it has not, we will see only his animality. To the vulgar, Falstaff will be forever just vulgar.

The problem of Falstaff himself cannot be separated from the problem of the fascination he exercises over us. Critics have long since put their fingers on the negative side of that secret. Half his charm resides in the fact that he is what we long to be and are not: *free.* Hence our delight in projecting on him our frustrated longing for emancipation. It is right here that those who do not like Falstaff score a cheap victory over those who do. The latter, say the former, are repressed or sedentary souls who go on a vicarious spree in the presence of one who commits all the sins they would like to commit but do not dare to. Like some of Falstaff's own hypotheses, the idea has an air of plausibility. But it involves a pitifully superficial view of Falstaff—as if his essence lay in his love of sack! No! it is for liberation from what all men want to be rid of, not just the bloodless few, that Falstaff stands: liberation from the tyranny of things as they are. Falstaff is immortal because he is a symbol of the supremacy of imagination over fact. He forecasts man's final victory over Fate itself. Facts stand in our way. Facts melt before Falstaff like ice before a summer sun—dissolve in the *aqua regia* of his resourcefulness and wit. He realizes the age-old dream of all men: to awaken in the morning and to know that no master, no employer, no bodily need or sense of duty calls, no fear or obstacle stands in the way— only a fresh beckoning day that is wholly ours.

But we have all awakened that way on rare occasions without becoming Falstaffs. Some men often do. An untrammeled day is not enough; we must have something to fill it with—besides lying in bed. Freedom is only the negative side of Falstaff. Possessing it, he perpetually does something creative with it. It is not enough for him to be the sworn enemy of facts. Any lazy man or fool is that. He is the sworn enemy of the factual spirit itself, of whatever is dull, inert, banal. Facts merely exist—and so do most men. Falstaff lives. And where he is, life becomes bright, active, enthralling.

Who has not been a member of some listless group on whom time has been hanging heavy when in the twinkling of an eye a newcomer has altered the face of everything as utterly as the sun, breaking through the clouds, transforms the surface of a gray lake? Boredom is banished. Gaiety is restored. The most apathetic member of the company is laughing and alert and will shortly be contributing his share to the flow of good spirits. What has done it? At bottom, of course, the mysterious fluid of an infectious personality. But so far as it can be analyzed, some tall tale or personal adventure wherein a grain of fact has been worked up with a pound of fiction, some impudent assumption about the host or absurd charge against somebody present rendered plausible by a precarious resemblance to the truth. Always *something made out of nothing*, with power, when added to the facts, to get the better of them. Never an unadulterated lie, but always some monstrous perversion, some scandalous interpretation, of what actually happened. An invention, yes, but an invention attached to reality by a thread of truth—the slenderer the better, so long as it does not break. What is Falstaff but an aggrandized, universalized, individualized version of this familiar phenomenon? He makes life again worth living.

And so, whether we approach Falstaff from the mythological or the psychological angle, we reach the same goal.

But alas! we have been neglecting the other Falstaff, the old sot. Unluckily—or perhaps luckily—there is another side to the story. Having fallen in love with Falstaff, we may now "stop to think" about him without compunction. And on examining more closely this symbol of man's supremacy over nature we perceive that he is not invulnerable. He has his Achilles heel. I do not refer to his love of Hal. That is his Achilles heel in another and lovelier sense. I refer to a tiny fact, two tiny facts, that he forgets and that we would like to: the fact that his imagination is stimulated by immense potations of sack and that his victories are purchased, if necessary, at the price of an utter disregard for the rights of others. We do not remember this until we stop to think. And we do not want to stop to think. We want to identify ourselves with the Immortal Falstaff. Yet there the Immoral Falstaff is all the while. And he must be reckoned with. Shakespeare was too much of a realist to leave him out.

The Greeks incarnated in their god Dionysus the paradox of wine, its combined power to inspire and degrade. *The Bacchae* of Euripides is the profoundest treatment of this theme in Hellenic if not in any literature. "No one can hate drunkenness more than I do," says Samuel Butler, "but I am confident the human intellect owes its superiority over that of the lower animals in great measure to the stimulus which alcohol has given to imagination—imagination being little else than another name for illusion." (It is usually presumptuous to disagree with Samuel Butler's use of words. But if he had substituted "mind" for "intellect" in the foregoing quotation I think he would have been nearer the mark. And only the unwary reader will think that by "illusion" Butler means the same thing as delusion or lie.) "The sway of alcohol over mankind," says William James, "is unquestionably due to its power to stimulate the mystical faculties of human nature [the imagination, that is, in its quintessence], usually crushed to earth by the cold facts and dry criticisms of the sober hour. Sobriety diminishes, discriminates, and says no; drunkenness expands, unites, and says yes. It is in fact the great exciter of the *Yes* function in man . . . it is part of the deeper mystery and tragedy of life that whiffs and gleams of something that we immediately recognize as excellent should be vouchsafed to so many of us only in the fleeting earlier phases of what in its totality is so degrading a poisoning."

James's contrast between the earlier and the later phases of alcoholic intoxication inevitably suggests the degeneration that Falstaff undergoes in the second part of *Henry IV*. That degeneration is an actual one, though several recent critics have tended to exaggerate it. Dover Wilson thinks that Shakespeare is deliberately trying to make us fall out of love with Falstaff so that we may accept with good grace his rejection by the new king. If so, for many readers he did not succeed very well. (Of that in its place.)

It is significant that we never see Falstaff drunk. His wit still scintillates practically unabated throughout the second part of the play, though some critics seem set on not admitting it. He is in top form, for instance, in this interview with the Chief Justice, and, to pick a single example from many, the reply he gives to John of Lancaster's reproach,

When everything is ended, then you come,

is one of his pinnacles: "Do you think me a swallow, an arrow, or a bullet?" No, the degeneration of Falstaff is not so much in his wit or even in his imagination as in his moral sensibility. The company he keeps grows more continuously low, and his treatment of Shallow and of his recruits shows an increasing hardness of heart. Shakespeare inserts too many little realistic touches to let us take these scenes as pure farce, and while no one in his senses would want to turn this aspect of the play into a temperance tract

it seems at times like an almost scientifically faithful account of the effect
of an excess of alcohol on the moral nature. In view of what Shakespeare
was at this time on the verge of saying about drunkenness in *Hamlet* and
of what he was to say about it later in *Othello, Antony and Cleopatra*, and
The Tempest, it is certain that he was profoundly interested in the subject;
and it is not far-fetched to suppose that he had in the back of his mind in
portraying the "degeneration" of Falstaff the nemesis that awaits the arti-
ficially stimulated mind. If so, the fat knight is Shakespeare's contribution,
in a different key, to the same problem that is treated in *The Bacchae*, and
his conclusions are close to those at which Euripides arrives.

VII

And then there is *The Merry Wives of Windsor*. (Here appears to be the
right place for a brief interlude on that play.) Criticism has been much
concerned over the connection, if any, between the Falstaff of *The Merry
Wives* and the Falstaff of *Henry IV*—with something like a consensus that
with the exception of a few dying sparks of the original one this is another
man. Yet one like between the two Falstaffs cannot be denied: with respect
to wit and resourcefulness they are exact opposites. The Falstaff we admire
is an incarnation of readiness; this one of helplessness. Nothing is too much
for the former. Anything is too much for the latter. They are, respectively,
presence and absence of mind. Such an utter antithesis is itself a connection.
Shakespeare must have meant something by it.

Nearly everyone is acquainted with the tradition that *The Merry Wives
of Windsor* was written in a fortnight at the command of Queen Elizabeth,
who wished to see the fat man in love. Shakespeare does appear to have
"tossed off" this sparkling farce-comedy, his one play of purely contemporary life and of almost pure prose, and, along with *The Comedy of Errors*,
his most inconsequential and merely theatrical one. Several hypotheses, or
some combination of them, may account for the Falstaff of this play.

Poets, as distinct from poets laureate, do not like commissions. It would
be quite like Shakespeare, ordered by the Queen to write another play about
Falstaff, to have his playful revenge by writing one about another man
entirely, under the same name. That was precisely the sort of thing that
Chaucer did when commanded by another Queen to write a *Legend of Good
Women*. It is fun to make a fool of royalty. Then, too, the conditions under
which the play was written, if the tradition is true, practically compelled
it to keep close to farce. And farce is the very atmosphere in which parody
thrives. This Falstaff is a kind of parody of the other one. But the closer

Shakespeare gets to farce, fancy, or nonsense, as he proves over and over, the more certain he is to have some serious underintention. On that principle, what better place than *The Merry Wives of Windsor* in which to insert an oblique comment on the Falstaff of *Henry IV*? Be that as it may, the Falstaff of this play is, as we said, an almost perfect picture, in exaggerated form and in a farcical key, of the Immortal Falstaff of the other plays, the old wretch of Bernard Shaw. Only the light tone of the piece keeps him from being "besotted and disgusting" also. Critics have seriously tried to determine at what spot chronologically this play should be inserted in the Henry series. Such an attempt betrays a curious ignorance of the ways of the imagination. But, after all due discount for the farce and fooling, the Falstaff of *The Merry Wives* looks like pretty good natural history of the latter end of an "old soak." From him it is a relief to get back, after our interlude, to the Immortal Falstaff, who, however entangled with the Immoral Falstaff, as the soul is with the body, breathes another and more transcendental air.

VIII

Is there any activity of man that involves the same factors that we find present in this Falstaff: complete freedom, an all-consuming zest for life, an utter subjugation of facts to imagination, and an entire absence of moral responsibility? Obviously there is. That activity is play.

Except for that little item of moral responsibility, "play" expresses as nearly as one word can the highest conception of life we are capable of forming: life for its own sake, life as it looks in the morning to a boy with

> no more behind
> But such a day to-morrow as to-day,
> And to be boy eternal,

life for the fun of it, as against life for what you can get out of it—or whom you can knock out of it. "Play" says what the word "peace" tries to say and doesn't. "Play" brings down to the level of everyone's understanding what "imagination" conveys to more sophisticated minds. For the element of imagination is indispensable to true play. Play is not sport. The confusion of the two is a major tragedy of our time. A crowd of fifteen-year-old schoolboys "playing" football on a back lot are indulging in sport. They are rarely playing. The one who is playing is the child of five, all alone, pretending that a dirty rag doll is the rich mother of a dozen infants— invisible to the naked eye. Even boys playing war, if they are harmonious and happy, are conducting an experiment in peace. Play is the erection of an illusion into a reality. It is not an escape from life. It is the realization of life in something like its fulness. What it *is* an escape from is the boredom and friction of existence. Like poetry, to which it is the prelude, it stands for a converting or winning-over of facts on a basis of friendship, the dissolving of them in a spirit of love, in contrast with science (at least the science of our day), which, somewhat illogically, stands first for recognition of the absolute autonomy of facts and then for their impressment and subjection to human demands by a kind of military conquest.

Now Falstaff goes through life playing. He coins everything he encounters into play, often even into *a* play. He would rather have the joke on himself and make the imaginative most of it than to have it on the other fellow and let the fun stop there. Whenever he seems to be taken in because he does not realize the situation, it is safer to assume that he does realize it but keeps quiet because the imaginative possibilities are greater in that case.

Watching him, we who in dead earnest have been attending to business or doing what we are pleased to call our duty suddenly realize what we have been missing. "The object of a man's life," says Robert Henri, "should be to play as a little child plays." If that is so we have missed the object of life, while Falstaff has attained it, or at least not missed it completely, as we have. It is his glory that, like Peter Pan, he never grew up, and that glory is the greater because he is an old man. As his immense size and weight were utilized by Shakespeare as a foil for the lightness of his spirit, so his age is used to stress its youthfulness. "You that are old," he says to the Chief Justice, who has been berating him for misleading the Prince, "consider not the capacities of us that are young." The Chief Justice replies that Falstaff is in every part "blasted with antiquity," his belly increasing in size, his voice broken, "and will you yet call yourself young? Fie, fie, fie, Sir John!" Falstaff retorts that as for his belly, he was born with a round one; as for his voice, he has lost it hollaing and singing of anthems; and as for his age, he is old only in judgment and understanding. Though the Lord Chief Justice has all the facts on his side, Falstaff has the victory. There has seldom been a more delicious interview.

As this scene suggests, the right way to take the Falstaff whom we love is to take him as a child. Mrs. Quickly did that in her immortal account of his death: he went away, she said, "an it had been any christom child." To call him a liar and let it go at that is like being the hardheaded father of a poetic little son who punishes him for falsehood when he has only been relating genuine imaginative experiences—as Blake's father thrashed him for saying he had seen angels in a tree. And to call him a coward and let it go at that is being no profounder.

But if it is the glory of the Immortal Falstaff that he remained a child, it is the shame of the Immoral Falstaff that he never became a man—for it is a child's duty to become a man no less than it is a man's duty to become a child. Falstaff detoured manhood instead of passing through it into a higher childhood. He is like the character in *The Pilgrim's Progress* who tried to steal into Paradise by climbing over the wall near its entrance instead of passing through the wicket gate and undergoing the trials that is the lot of man to endure. He wanted the victory without paying the price. He wanted to be an individual regardless of the social consequences, to persist in the prerogatives of youth without undertaking the responsibilities of maturity. But if his virtues are those of a child rather than those of a man, that does not prevent him from being immensely superior to those in these plays who possess the virtues of neither man nor child, or from giving us gleams of a life beyond good and evil.

Dover Wilson (following Professor R. A. Law) would have us take *Henry IV* as a morality play wherein a madcap prince grows up into an ideal king. Falstaff is the devil who tempts the Prince to Riot. Hotspur and especially the Lord Chief Justice are the good angels representing Chivalry and Justice or the Rule of Law. It is a struggle between Vanity and Government for the possession of the Royal Prodigal.

The scheme is superbly simple and as moral as a Sunday-school lesson. But it calmly leaves the Immortal Falstaff quite out of account! If Falstaff were indeed just the immoral creature that in part he admittedly is, Wilson's parable would be more plausible, though even then the words he picks to characterize Falstaff are singularly unfortunate. "Vanity" by derivation means emptiness or absence of substance, and "riot" quarrelsomeness. Imagine calling even the Immoral Falstaff empty or lacking in substance— or quarrelsome! He had his vices but they were not these. For either vanity or riot there is not a single good word to be said. To equate Falstaff with them is to assert that not a single good word can be said for him—a preposterous proposition. Wit, humor, laughter, good-fellowship, insatiable zest for life: are these vanity or does Falstaff not embody them? That is the dilemma in which Mr. Wilson puts himself. And as for the Lord Chief Justice, he is indeed an admirable man; a more incorruptible one in high position is not to be found in Shakespeare. But if the poet had intended to assign him any such crucial role as Mr. Wilson thinks, he certainly would have presented him more fully and would have hesitated to let Falstaff make him look so foolish. For the Chief Justice's sense of justice was better developed than his sense of humor. And even justice is not all.

Henry IV does have a certain resemblance to a morality play. The two, however, between whom the younger Henry stands and who are in a sense contending for the possession of his soul are not Falstaff and the Chief Justice, but Falstaff and the king. It is between Falstaff and the Father—to use that work in its generic sense—that Henry finds himself.

Now in the abstract this is indeed Youth between Revelry and Responsibility. But the abstract has nothing to do with it. Where Henry really stands is between this particular companion, Falstaff, and this particular father and king, Henry IV. Of the two, which was the better man?

Concede the utmost—that is, take Falstaff at his worst. He was a drunkard, a glutton, a profligate, a thief, even a liar if you insist, but withal a fundamentally honest man. He had two sides like a coin, but he was not a counterfeit. And Henry? He was a king, a man of "honour," of brains and ability, of good intentions, but withal a "vile politician" and respectable hypocrite. He *was* a counterfeit. Which, if it comes to the choice, is the better influence on a young man? Shakespeare, for one, gives no evidence of having an iota of doubt.

But if even Falstaff at his worst comes off better than Henry, how about Falstaff at his best? In that case, what we have is Youth standing between Imagination and Authority, between Freedom and Force, between Play and War. My insistence that Falstaff is a double man, and that the abstract has nothing to do with it, will acquit me of implying that this is the whole of the story. But it is a highly suggestive part of it.

The opposite of war is not "peace" in the debased sense in which we are in the habit of using the latter word. Peace ought to mean far more, but what it has come to mean on our lips is just the absence of war. The opposite of war is creative activity, play in its loftier implications. All through these dramas the finer Falstaff symbolizes the opposite of force. When anything military enters his presence, it instantly looks ridiculous and begins to shrink. Many methods have been proposed for getting rid of war. Falstaff's is one of the simplest: laugh it out of existence. For war is almost as foolish as it is criminal. "Laugh it out of existence?" If only we could! Which is the equivalent of saying: if only more of us were like Falstaff! These plays should be required reading in all military academies. Even the "cannon-fodder" scenes of Falstaff with his recruits have their serious implications and anticipate our present convictions on the uneugenic nature of war.

How far did Shakespeare sympathize with Falstaff's attitude in this matter? No one is entitled to say. But much further, I am inclined to think, than he would have had his audience suspect or than the world since his time has been willing to admit. For consider the conditions under which Falstaff finds himself:

Henry has dethroned and murdered the rightful king of England. The Percys have developed him to obtain the crown, but a mutual sense of guilt engenders distrust between the two parties, and the Percys decide to dethrone the dethroner. Falstaff is summoned to take part in his defense. "Life is given but once." Why should Falstaff risk his one life on earth, which he is enjoying as not one man in a hundred million does, to support or to oppose the cause of either of two equally selfish and equally damnable seekers after power and glory? What good would the sacrifice of his life accomplish comparable to the boon that he confers daily and hourly on the world, to say nothing of himself, by merely being? This is no case of tyranny on one side and democracy on the other, with the liberty or slavery of a world at stake. This is a strictly dynastic quarrel. When two gangs of gunmen begin shooting it out on the streets of a great city, the discreet citizen will step behind a post or into a doorway. The analogy may not be an exact one, but it enables us to understand Falstaff's point of view. And there is plenty of Shakespearean warrant for it.

> See the coast clear'd, and then we will depart,

says the Mayor of London when caught, in *1 Henry VI*, between similar brawling factions,

> Good God! these nobles should such stomachs bear;
> I myself fight not once in forty year.

And Mercutio's "A plague o' both your houses!" comes to mind. Shakespeare meant more by that phrase than the dying man who coined it could have comprehended.

"But how about Falstaff's honor?" it will be asked. "Thou owest God a death," says the prince to him before the battle of Shrewsbury. " 'Tis not due yet," Falstaff answers as Hal goes out,

> I would be loath to pay him before his day. What need I be so forward with him that calls not on me? Well, 'tis no matter; honour pricks me on. Yea, but how if honour prick me off when I came on? how then? Can honour set to a leg? No. Or an arm? No. Or take away the grief of a wound? No. Honour hath no skill in surgery, then? No. What is honour? A word. What is in that word honour? What is that honour? Air; a trim reckoning! Who hath it? He that died o' Wednesday. Doth he feel it? No. Doth he hear it? No. 'Tis insensible, then? Yea, to the dead. But will it not live with the living? No. Why? Detraction will not suffer it. Therefore I'll none of it. Honour is a mere scutcheon: and so ends my catechism.

"You must be honorable to talk of honor," says a character in *A Raw Youth*, "or, if not, all you say is a lie." The word "honor," as that sentence of Dostoevsky's shows, is still an honorable word. It can still mean, and could in Shakespeare's day, the integrity of the soul before God. The Chief Justice had honor in that sense. But "honour" in its decayed feudal sense of glory, fame, even reputation, as page after page of these Chronicle Plays records, had outlived its usefulness and the time had come to expose its hollowness. The soul, lifted up, declared Saint Teresa (who died in 1582), sees in the word "honor" "nothing more than an immense lie of which the world remains a victim . . . She laughs when she sees grave persons, persons of orison, caring for points of honor for which she now feels profoundest contempt . . . With what friendship we would all treat each other if our interest in honor and in money could but disappear from the earth! For my own part, I feel as if it would be a remedy for all our ills."

Saint Teresa and Sir John Falstaff! an odd pair to find in agreement— about honor if not about money. In the saint's case no ambiguity is attached to the doctrine that honor is a lie. In the sinner's, there remains something equivocal and double-edged. Here, if ever, the two Falstaffs meet. The grosser Falstaff is himself a parasite and a dishonorable man, and coming from him the speech is the creed of Commodity and the height of irony. But that does not prevent the man who loved Hal and babbled of green fields at his death from revealing in the same words, as clearly as Saint Teresa, that life was given for something greater than glory or than the gain that can be gotten out of it.

"Give me life," cries Falstaff on the field of Shrewsbury. "Die all, die merrily," cries Hotspur. That is the gist of it. The prince killed Hotspur in the battle, and Falstaff, with one of his most inspired lies, claimed the deed as his own. But Falstaff's lies, scrutinized, often turn out to be truth in disguise. So here. Falstaff, not Prince Henry, did kill Hotspur. He ended the outworn conception of honor for which Hotspur stood. The prince killed his body, but Falstaff killed his soul—or rather what passed for his soul.

The dying Hotspur himself sees the truth. The verdict of his final breath is that life is "time's fool" and he himself dust. And the prince, gazing down at his dead victim, sees it too, if only for a moment.

> Ill-weav'd ambition, how much art thou shrunk!
> When that this body did contain a spirit,
> A kingdom for it was too small a bound,

he exclaims, and, turning, he catches sight of another body from which life has also apparently departed:

> What, old acquaintance! could not all this flesh
> Keep in a little life? Poor Jack, farewell!
> I could have better spar'd a better man.

But nobody was ever more mistaken on this subject of life and flesh than was Henry on this occasion, as the shamming Falstaff proves a moment later, when the prince goes out, by rising from the dead. " 'Sblood," he cries,

> 'twas time to counterfeit, or that hot termagant Scot had paid me scot and lot too. Counterfeit? I lie, I am no counterfeit. To die is to be a counterfeit; for he is but the counterfeit of a man who hath not the life of a man; but to counterfeit dying, when a man thereby liveth, is to be no counterfeit, but the true and perfect image of life indeed. The better part of valour is discretion.

> I fear thou art another counterfeit,

Douglas had cried, coming on Henry IV on the field of Shrewsbury,

> Another king! they grow like Hydra's heads.
> I am the Douglas, fatal to all those
> That wear those colours on them. What art thou,
> That counterfeit'st the person of a king?

The literal reference of course is to the knights, disguised to represent the king, that Henry had sent into the battle to divert the enemy from his own person. "The better part of valour is discretion." This, and that repeated word "counterfeit," is Shakespeare's sign that he intends the contrast, and the deeper unconscious meaning of Douglas'

> What art thou,
> That counterfeit'st the person of a king?

(a king, notice, not the king) is just one more of the poet's judgments upon Henry. For all his "discretion," the Douglas would have killed this counterfeit king who tries to save his skin by the death of others if the prince had not come to his rescue in the nick of time.

But that was earlier in the battle. At the point we had reached the prince comes back with his brother John and discovers the "dead" Falstaff staggering along with the dead Hotspur on his back—a symbolic picture if there ever was one.

> Did you not tell me this fat man was dead?

cries Lancaster.

> I did; I saw him dead,
> Breathless and bleeding on the ground,

replies Henry. He has underrated the vitality of the Imagination, and even now thinks he sees a ghost:

> Art thou alive?
> Or is it fantasy that plays upon our eyesight?
> I prithee, speak; we will not trust our eyes
> Without our ears. Thou art not what thou seem'st.

"No: that's certain," retorts Falstaff, "I am not a double man." And to prove it, he throws down the body of Hotspur he is carrying. But beyond this obvious meaning, who can doubt that Falstaff, in the phrase "double man," is also having a thrust at the dual role of the man he is addressing, or that Shakespeare, in letting Falstaff deny his own doubleness, is thereby calling our attention to it? At the very least the expression proves that the world did not have to wait for Dostoevsky before it heard of the double man.

Truth has made it necessary to say some harsh things about Prince Henry; so it is a pleasure to recognize the character of his conduct on the field of Shrewsbury: his valor in his encounter with Hotspur, his courage and loyalty in rescuing his father from Douglas, and his generosity in letting Falstaff take credit for Hotspur's death. Dover Wilson makes much of this last point—too much, I think, for the good of his own case—declaring that it proves the prince thought nothing of renown, of "the outward show of honour in the eyes of men, so long as he has proved himself worthy of its inner substance in his own." But if he was as self-effacing as all that, why did he cry at the moment he met Hotspur?—

> all the budding honours on thy crest
> I'll crop, to make a garland for my head.

Those words flatly contradict the "grace" he does Falstaff in surrendering to him so easily the greatest honor of his life. The paradox arises, I think, from the presence of those conflicting personalities, Hal and the prince. Touched momentarily at the sight of what he believes to be his old companion dead at his feet, the fast-disappearing Hal returns and survives long enough after the surprise and joy of finding him still alive to accept Falstaff's lie for truth. But we wonder how much longer. Wilson's assumption that the prince would or could have kept up the fiction permanently is refuted by the fact that Morton had observed the death of Hotspur at Henry's hands and reports the event correctly:

> these mine eyes saw him in bloody state,
> Rendering faint quittance, wearied and outbreath'd,
> To Harry Monmouth; whose swift wrath beat down
> The never-daunted Percy to the earth,
> From whence with life he never more sprung up.

Everything, from the famous first soliloquy on, proves that the prince not only craved renown but craved it in its most theatrical form.

Falstaff and Don Quixote

Wyndham Lewis

"The wound that phantom gave me!" is an exclamation illustrating the quixotic attitude to the environing world, which, if it lends qualities to things they do not possess, restores in a sense the balance by not bestowing on any existence quite the harshness of the analytic eye of common sense. Don Quixote is of course one of the many demented characters inhabiting the region of great fiction. Hamlet, Lear, Othello, Timon are all demented or hallucinated, as so many of the celebrated figures in nineteenth-century Russian fiction were. It is the supreme liberty that it is possible to take with your material. That it should be so often taken in the case of the great characters of dramatic fiction is the most evident testimony to the dependence on untruth, in every sense, in which our human nature and human environment put us. In the case of Muishkin, Dostoevsky had to call in express and abnormal physiological conditions to help him incarnate his saint. And the natural heightening everywhere in Shakespeare is by way of madness. Since it is mad to behave in the way the hero does, he has to be maddened by some means or other more often than not in order to make him at all probable.

"The defeat of the hero" to see "the splendid triumph of his heroism" is in accord with the definitely tragic nature of the jest, and the movement of thought beneath the symbolization. That Don Quixote has not a ceremonious pathos, and that he only fights with phantoms which we know under homely shapes, does not make him any less a hero. Though Persiles and Sigismunda, for instance, could easily be confounded with the conventional heroes of Heliodorus—similarly connected with Thessaly—Don Quixote is, in literature, a lonely hero, and even in that responds to one of the chief requirements of tragedy, approximating at the same time to one of the conditions of madness.

The effect of Cervantes on the German romantics—G. Schlegel Tieck and Schelling—produced some interesting results. Some of their conclusions appear to me to correspond to the truth of the figure of Don Quixote.

"Schelling put into definite shape the formula of the new interpretation: he saw in *Don Quixote* the philosophical novel par excellence, in the great adventure of Quixote the universal conflict of the ideal and the real, and in the defeat of the hero the triumph of his heroism."

"For the rest, *Don Quixote*, interpretated from the romantic point of view, was in no way opposed to the spirit of adventure and mystical dreams, rather it exalted sacrifice and devotion to the Idea, and thus favoured every kind of religious and political initiative. And, on the other hand, romantic irony found in the spectacle of the eternal duality suggested by Don Quixote the justification of its smile and of its lofty detachment" (J. J. Bertrand).

You must not, the German romantics said, see in *Don Quixote* simply a good after-dinner laugh, a *bambocciata*.

"In the theory of universal discord, the principle [of the interpretation] is to be found. Schiller had adopted the hypothesis of the primordial disunity of the world, the result of which is the tragic antithesis in which we are struggling. Fichte opposed still more violently the self and not-self, and made familiar to contemporary thought this system of antagonism between life and the dream, the trivial and the ideal. Don Quixote is the symbol of this duality."

Such "romantic" explanations appear to be the only ones compatible with the great beauty of this book.

It was perhaps the long stay Cervantes made in Italy that enabled him to look at Spanish life with detached and foreign eyes: but being an artist can alone have produced this condition in Shakespeare. And I think there is nothing in Shakespeare's work that makes him so national as Cervantes was. Shakespeare's laborious—and in a small business way, successful—life was not a fierce and youthful episode, like Marlowe's. But he had his share of hardness and effectiveness: which again, if you regard it as the most exterior thing, and if you wished to trace it to the influence of an environment, would be natural to people living in a great and noisy town, in the midst of affairs, and of a rapidly changing life. Whereas Cervantes had the idyllic peace of the grave landscapes of his country as a background, and had round him the gentler agricultural life of a "backward" people.

According to Kyd, Marlowe was "irreligious . . . intemperate, and of a cruel heart." He was involved in seditious movements, was considered hostile to religion and died in a brawl. Raleigh's departure in search of El Dorado followed religious persecution and espionage. Marlowe was caught up in the atmosphere of plots and heroics of which that is an example. Kyd attributes to Marlowe a document for which he, Kyd, was arrested, and which is described as a "libell that concerned the State." It was apparently the text of a placard (described by the register of the Privy Council as *a lewd and mutinous libell*) of which some had been stuck upon the wall of the Dutch churchyard. It is as well to remember on all counts that Shakespeare was very much influenced by Marlowe, and shared probably some, at least, of his habits and opinions.

Whether Falstaff (Shakespeare's "knight," as Don Quixote was Cervantes') was only a whimsical invention to amuse; or how far certain more fundamental things—and what things—were involved, has, like most of the matters connected with this very rich and complex work—overcrowded with startlingly real figures—been much discussed. Ulrici, for example, thinks that *The Merry Wives* is a satire, from the bourgeois point of view, on chivalry—Falstaff representing chivalry:

"The burgher class avenges itself pretty severely upon Falstaff's knighthood, and his knighthood does not anywhere appear more miserable and unknightly than when thrown into a basket among dirty clothes, when beaten as an old woman and tormented and pinched as a fantastic satyr. In fact, it seems to me that these three features might be found to contain as many metaphorico-satirical thrusts at the chivalry of the day."

Possibly every class—as it is supposed that every type of man—found its expression in this universal poet, and the new *magnificos* of London and the Italianized courtier, and even the many-headed beast, could find something to please them. But with that mechanical type of criticism that could see in a figure like Falstaff the expression of a class it is difficult to agree.

Where Ulrici says that Falstaff is the "impersonification of the whole of this refined and artificial civilization"—and more closely still that he is a child, a *naïf*—he has, I think, established one of the important things about him. To this I will presently return.

This passage of Ulrici on Falstaff is, in full, as follows:

"He is, so to say, the symbol, the personification of that general state of human frailty which, without being actually wicked—that is, without doing evil for the sake of evil, in order to find satisfaction in it—nevertheless perpetually does evil (to a certain extent against his will) simply because it happens to be the most direct means of attaining what he calls life and happiness; this, he believes, is not only actually arrived at by everyone, but ought to be allowed to be the aim of everyone. In so far Falstaff is a pure child of nature, and it cannot be denied that in *Henry IV*, at least, he shows some sparks of that *naïveté*, gay humour and innocent good-nature, which is generally peculiar to the so-called children of nature; but he is a child of nature who not only stands in the midst of, on many sides, an advanced state of civilization, but who—owing to the refined luxury of his enjoyments, the variety of his dissolute appetites, and the manifold devices he makes use of to gratify them—is, at the same time, the impersonification of the whole of this refined and artificial civilization."

If you imagine Shakespeare taking Falstaff all through his plays—or through as many more as possible—then we should have, still more, a central and great figure (which would also be an *idea*) to place beside Cervantes' knight.

"These scenes [the comic Falstaffian ones in *Henry IV*] fill almost one half of the whole play. In no other historical drama of Shakespeare's do we find such a total disregard of the subject. Here . . . the comic and unhistorical portions are so surprisingly elaborate, that the question as to their justification becomes a vital point . . ."

It was not, according to Ulrici, "Shakespeare's intention merely to give a broader foil to the character of Prince Henry." Nor can it have been "Shakespeare's intention in *Henry IV* merely to give a representation of the return of honour and of man's different ideas and positions in regard to it; and he has assuredly not introduced the representatives of the idea of honour—the Prince and Percy—with Falstaff, the negative counterpart, the caricature of honour and knighthood" (Ulrici, book 6, chap. 7).

Ulrici's solution is that the comic is set to dog the historic in *Henry IV* on purpose to show up its influence: "It is intended to parody the hollow pathos of the political history [i.e., of Henry IV's reign] . . . Irony is to hold up its concave mirror to that mere semblance of history which is so frequently mistaken for history itself, as being considered great and important only when it parades about in its purple mantle with crown and sceptre, haggles about kingdoms, or lays about it with the scourge of war. For all that which in the present drama appears outwardly to be historical action—rebellion, dissension, and war, victory and defeat, the critics of political cunning, treaties and negotiations with their high-sounding speeches about right and wrong—all this was in truth a mere show, the mere mark of history. The reign was of historical importance only as a transition stage in the further development of the great historical tragedy, and accordingly could not be passed over."

So "to give a clear exhibition of this unreality [that of the proceedings of the 'born actor' Bolingbroke and his playful barons] this semblance, this histrionic parade, was—conveniently or inconveniently—the poet's intention in placing the comic scenes so immediately by the side of the historical action, and in allowing them step by step to accompany the course of the latter."

Ulrici thinks that the contrast was necessary only because of the emptiness of this *particular* history, in short. It is very easy, in view of the so-called enigmatical play of *Troilus and Cressida*, and in the view upheld here of a great many other points in all the plays, to *extend* this estimate of Ulrici to the whole of Shakespeare's works.

I will now show how all these various questions we have passed in review during the last few chapters can be combined, and how they each contribute to fixing a psychical centre of control which is responsible for all of them. First of all, what I named *shamanization* must be reverted to: its effects will be found a necessary ingredient of one of the most celebrated attributes of Shakespeare—namely, his humour. How "worldliness" which we have discussed [elsewhere]—comes in always on the feminine tide of feeling is evident; and how scepticism is not incompatible with courage, any more than it is with feminineness—indeed the contrary, since the female animal is very brave, but on account of different things to the male.

For those who are not familiar with the phenomenon of shamanization, still universally prevalent among the subarctic tribes, I will briefly describe it.

A shaman is a person following the calling of a magician or priest: and the word shamanization that I have employed would refer to a shaman (the most typical of them) who had in addition transformed himself. This phenomenon—that of sex-transformation—in our life to-day is so evident, and so widespread, that (unless we are never to refer at all to a thing that exercises such great social influence, and whose prevalence in one manner or another, principally by way of social suggestion, affects the general outlook on life) we should find some cliché that does not smell of the laboratory, or some word that does not belong to those latinizing vulgarities of speech depended on for popular discussion. On behalf of the word employed I have no ambitious views: it is only an inoffensive and convenient counter for my personal use; and because around the figure of the shaman I have elsewhere gathered a number of observations on this subject, and it has naturally suggested itself to me in the course of use.

As to the phenomenon itself, of sexual perversion, I am not one of those people who regard it as insignificant, or harmless as a widespread fashion: though it is so very much involved with other things (which on the surface seem to have little to do with it) that it is meaningless to discuss it by itself. Its manifestations and effects are extremely different in different ages and countries: successful in Sparta, in Lesbos it might be an offence, and in Chicago a useless and unornamental one, where it would probably take on a curious mechanical intensity, and an earnest scientific air. It might add charm to the south of Russia, but make the arctic rigours of the north still more unendurable. In Rome, for example, its effects were coarse and disagreeable, whereas in Athens they even had the intellect as an ally, recommending them. These general reflections on the nature of perversion do not concern us here very much, except that it seemed advisable to record that partiality for its numerous adepts, and its effects as revealed in current social life, cannot be attributed to me.

Shamanism, then, returning to the custom prevalent throughout the north of Asia and America, consists generally in the reversal of sex: a man, feeling himself unsuited for his sex, dresses himself as a woman, behaves as a woman (usually adopting the woman's rôle also where some man is concerned), or by means of this sexual abnegation prepares himself for the duties of a magician. Women similarly abandon the outward attributes of sex and become men. (This is more rare, because it is obviously a less attractive proposition—and this does not take with it properly an enhancement of the powers of "mystery," as the other transformation does.)

Generally speaking, the process of shamanizing himself confers on a man the feminine advantages. It signifies either a desire to experience the sensual delights peculiar to the female organization; or else an ambition to identify himself with occult powers. But it is further a withdrawal from masculine responsibilities in every sense, and an adoption of the spectator's rôle of the woman (freed further, in his case, from the cares of motherhood). That this is a very radical and even inversely heroic, or heroically inverse, proceeding is evident. If we now turn to a figure with which we have already dealt—namely, the "man of the world" (a figure with whom by implication Shakespeare is compromised, but from identification with whom this analysis should, in effect, rescue him)—we shall find that there is nothing that exactly corresponds to the transformed shaman. Like the latter, as it is his strategy to include among his numerous advantages those possessed by the woman, he has a tincture of the shaman in him. Hotspur (one of Shakespeare's lesser heroes) tells in a famous speech how he meets on the battlefield a shamanizing sprig of nobility, whom he describes as chiding soldiers carrying dead bodies near him "for bringing a slovenly unhandsome corpse between the wind and his nobility." This exquisite was not necessarily a wholly shamanized man, but possibly only a macaroni of the time. He would in that case be a "man of the world" of a very extravagant type, very extravagantly shamanized. He would have on the field of battle all the privileges of a woman, only frowned at—and perhaps hustled—by the blustering Percy.

It is at this point that, fully prepared, we can address ourselves to the subject that can be regarded as the centre one in Shakespeare—that of his *humour*.

The humour of Falstaff achieves the same magical result as Don Quixote's chivalrous delusion—namely, it makes him immune from its accidents. The battles he finds himself engaged in are jokes; his opponents, the Douglas, Colevile of the dale, are "phantoms" (of a different sort, it is true), just as Don Quixote's are. The contrast of these two knights is a contrast in two unrealities—two specifics to turn the world by enchantment into something else. One is the sense of humour, the other is the mysticism of chivalry; the first a negation, the latter a positive inspiration. The one, the magic of being wide awake (very wide awake—beyond normal common sense): the other of having your eyes naturally sealed up, and of dreaming.

The "sense of humour," again provides us with an exceptionally English or American attribute of worldliness.

In Falstaff, Shakespeare has given us a very interesting specimen indeed of consummate worldliness, with a very powerfully developed humorous proclivity, which served him better than any suit of armour could in the various vicissitudes of his life. An excellent substitute even for a shamanizing faculty, and enabling its possessor to escape the inconveniences and conventional disgrace of being feminine—at the same time it provides him with most of the social advantages of the woman. The sense of humour is from that point of view the masterpiece of worldly duplicity and strategy. On the field of battle at Tewkesbury, Falstaff avails himself of it in a famous scene, and gives us a classical exhibition of its many advantages, and the graceful operation of its deceit. It does not cut off its practitioner from "men" of the rough "hero type," but on the contrary endears him to them. So it becomes even a substitute for courage. There is no lack that is does not cover. With it Falstaff is as safe on the battlefield as the shamanized noble noticed by Percy Hotspur.

So if Falstaff is the embodiment of a mass of worldly expedient, this is of course all directed to defeating the reality as much as Don Quixote's. He is a walking disease, but his disease is used to evade the results of that absence of a sense of humour which is so conspicuous a characteristic of nature and natural phenomena. The sense of humour is woven into a magic carpet; with it he progresses through his turbulent career, bearing a charmed life. This "sense" performs for Falstaff the office of a psychological liberator; it is of magic potency, turning the field of Tewkesbury into a field of play, and cheating death wherever they meet.

The man would indeed be a coward who, possessed of this magic, was seriously timid. Falstaff was evidently not that: yet Morgan thought it necessary to write a book defending his "honour" in this respect. "He had from nature," he said, "as I presume to say, a spirit of boldness and enterprise."

Being a humorous figure par excellence, it was not possible for him to brave in the hero's way, any more than it would be proper for the circus clown to be an obviously accomplished athlete. Gaucherie and laughable failure is, in both cases, of the essence of their rôle. But boldness and enterprise—as far as that was compatible with the necessity of advertising a lack of courage—he possessed to a great degree.

Morgan begins his defence of Falstaff's courage by appealing to the fact that actions (by which people usually judge character) are a very misleading key: "The understanding seems for the most part to take cognizance of actions only, and from these to infer motives and characters; but the sense we have been speaking of proceeds in a contrary direction."

So he appeals for the actions that were not there—and in the nature of things could not have been there—in his conventional pleading.

As to Falstaff being "a constitutional coward" (like Parolles or Bobadil) he says:

> The reader, I believe, would wonder extremely to find either Parolles or Bobadil possess himself in danger. What then can be the cause that we are not at all surprised at the gaiety and ease of Falstaff under the most trying circumstances; and that we never think of charging *Shakespeare* with departing, on that account, from the truth and coherence of character? Perhaps, after all, the real character of Falstaff may be different from his apparent one; and possibly this difference between reality and appearance, whilst it accounts at once for our liking and our censure, may be the true point of humour in the character, and the source of all our laughter and delight. We may chance to find, if we will but examine a little into the nature of those circumstances which have accidentally involved him, that he was intended to be drawn as a character of much natural courage and resolution; and be obliged thereupon to repeal these decisions.

Morgan's affected defence (of Falstaff's physical courage) is successfully achieved—but at the expense of every psychologic requirement of the case.

Morgan makes a point of Falstaff's freedom from malice: "He [Falstaff] seems by nature to have had a mind free of malice or any evil principle; but he never took the trouble of acquiring any good one. He found himself (from the start) esteemed and loved with all his faults, nay for his faults, which were all connected with humour, and for the most part grew out of it." So "laughter and approbation attend his greatest excesses."

This is of course the "man of the world" in Falstaff—the anti-Machiavel of the type of Frederick the Great. But the "good fellow" in Falstaff, as it is in anybody almost, was no more innocent than, actually not as innocent as, Machiavelli's "bad fellow" or male persona. There is, in short, much method in such sanity.

Morgan piles up his understandings of the plan of this character:

"We all like *Old Jack*; yet, by some strange perverse fate, we all abuse him, and deny him the possession of any one single good or respectable quality. There is something extraordinary in this; it must be a strange art in Shakespeare which can draw our liking and good will towards so offensive an object. He has wit, it will be said: cheerfulness and humour of the most characteristic and captivating sort. And is this enough? Is the humour and gaiety of vice so very captivating? Is the wit, characteristic of baseness and every ill quality, capable of attaching the heart or winning the affections! Or does not the apparency of such humour, and the flashes of such wit, by more strongly disclosing the deformity of character but the more strongly excite our hatred and contempt for the man?"

The nonsense into which the moralist critic leads the amiable eighteenth-century writer at least becomes palpable here—even if worthlessness does not become more palpable when associated with wit. That it is not good qualities, any more than great qualities, that "attach the heart" it is not necessary to say.

Falstaff is a "man of wit and pleasure," and could generally be described as a very good specimen of a "man of the world." But the same thing applies to him as to Iago: the "man of the world" is never so dramatically and openly cynical as Falstaff, any more than he is so candid as Machiavelli. He is not dramatic at all. To come to one of the necessary conclusions in this connexion, if the Machiavel were an Englishman he would be like Falstaff. This laziness, rascality and "good fellow" quality, crafty in the brainless animal way, is the English way of being a "deep-brained Machiavel."

But Falstaff is a "child," too, a "*naïf*," as Ulrici says. A worldly mixture of any strength is never without that ingredient. The vast compendium of worldly bluff that is Falstaff would have to contain that. It was like "any christom child" that he "went away," Mistress Quickly says.

He is armed from head to foot with sly feminine inferiorities, lovable weaknesses and instinctively cultivated charm. He is a big helpless bag of guts, exposing himself boldly to every risk on the child's, or the woman's, terms. When he runs away or lies down he is more adorable than any hero "facing fearful odds."

His immense girth and stature lends the greatest point, even, to his character. He is a hero run hugely to seed: he is actually heavier and bigger than the heaviest and biggest true colossus or hero. He is in that respect, physically, a mock-hero. Then this childishness is enhanced by his great physical scale, so much the opposite of the child's perquisite of smallness. And because of this meaningless, unmasculine immensity he always occupies the centre of the stage, he is the great landmark in any scene where he is. It all means nothing, and is a physical sham and trick put on the eye. And so he becomes the embodiment of bluff and worldly practice, the colossus of the little.

Rule and Misrule in *Henry IV, Part 1*

C. L. Barber

If all the year were playing holidays,
To sport would be as tedious as to work.

The two parts of *Henry IV*, written probably in 1597 and 1598, are an astonishing development of drama in the direction of inclusiveness, a development possible because of the range of the traditional culture and the popular theater, but realized only because Shakespeare's genius for construction matched his receptivity. We have noticed briefly [elsewhere] how, early in his career, Shakespeare made brilliant use of the long-standing tradition of comic accompaniment and counterstatement by the clown. Now suddenly he takes the diverse elements in the potpourri of the popular chronicle play and composes a structure in which they draw each other out. The Falstaff comedy, far from being forced into an alien environment of historical drama, is begotten by that environment, giving and taking meaning as it grows. The implications of the saturnalian attitude are more drastically and inclusively expressed here than anywhere else, because here misrule is presented along with rule and along with the tensions that challenge rule. Shakespeare dramatizes not only holiday but also the need for holiday and the need to limit holiday.

It is in the Henry IV plays that we can consider most fruitfully general questions concerning the relation of comedy to analogous forms of symbolic action in folk rituals: not only the likenesses of comedy to ritual, but the differences, the features of comic form which make it comedy and not ritual. Such analogies, I think, prove to be useful critical tools: they lead

From *Shakespeare's Festive Comedy: A Study of Dramatic Form and Its Relation to Social Custom*. © 1959 by Princeton University Press.

us to see structure in the drama. And they also raise fascinating historical and theoretical questions about the relation of drama to other products of culture. One way in which our time has been seeing the universal in literature has been to find in complex literary works patterns which are analogous to myths and rituals and which can be regarded as archetypes, in some sense primitive or fundamental. I have found this approach very exciting indeed. But at the same time, such analysis can be misleading if it results in equating the literary form with primitive analogues. When we are dealing with so developed an art as Shakespeare's, in so complex an epoch as the Renaissance, primitive patterns may be seen in literature mainly because literary imagination, exploiting the heritage of literary form, disengages them from the suggestions of a complex culture. And the primitive levels are articulated in the course of reunderstanding their nature—indeed, the primitive can be fully expressed only on condition that the artist can deal with it in a most civilized way. Shakespeare presents patterns analogous to magic and ritual in the process of redefining magic as imagination, ritual as social action.

Shakespeare was the opposite of primitivistic, for in his culture what we search out and call primitive was in the blood and bone as a matter of course; the problem was to deal with it, to master it. The Renaissance, moreover, was a moment when educated men were modifying a ceremonial conception of human life to create a historical conception. The ceremonial view, which assumed that names and meanings are fixed and final, expressed experience as pageant and ritual—pageant where the right names could march in proper order, or ritual where names could be changed in the right, the proper way. The historical view expresses life as drama. People in drama are not identical with their names, for they gain and lose their names, their status and meaning—and not by settled ritual: the gaining and losing of names, of meaning, is beyond the control of any set ritual sequence. Shakespeare's plays are full of pageantry and of action patterned in a ritualistic way. But the pageants are regularly interrupted; the rituals are abortive or perverted; or if they succeed, they succeed against odds or in an unexpected fashion. The people in the plays try to organize their lives by pageant and ritual, but the plays are dramatic precisely because the effort fails. This failure drama presents as history and personality; in the largest perspective, as destiny.

At the heart of the plays there is, I think, a fascination with the individualistic use or abuse of ritual—with magic. There is an intoxication with the possibility of an omnipotence of mind by which words might become things, by which a man might "gain a deity," might achieve, by making his own ritual, an unlimited power to incarnate meaning. This fascination is expressed in the poetry by which Shakespeare's people envisage their ideal selves. But his drama also expresses an equal and complementary awareness that magic is delusory, that words can become things or lead to deeds only within a social group, by virtue of a historical, social situation beyond the mind and discourse of any one man. This awareness of limitations is expressed by the ironies, whether comic or tragic, which Shakespeare embodies in the dramatic situations of his speakers, the ironies which bring down the meanings which fly high in winged words.

In using an analogy with temporary king and scapegoat to bring out patterns of symbolic action in Falstaff's role, it will be important to keep it clear that the analogy is one we make now, that it is not Shakespeare's analogy: otherwise we falsify his relation to tradition. He did not need to discriminate consciously, in our way, underlying configurations which came to him with his themes and materials. His way of extending consciousness of such patterns was the drama. In creating the Falstaff comedy, he fused two main saturnalian traditions, the clowning customary on the stage and the folly customary on holiday, and produced something unprecedented. He was working out attitudes towards chivalry, the state and crown in history, in response to the challenge posed by the fate he had dramatized in *Richard II*. The fact that we find analogies to the ritual interregnum relevant to what Shakespeare produced is not the consequence of a direct influence; his power of dramatic statement, in developing saturnalian comedy, reached to modes of organizing experience which primitive cultures have developed with a clarity of outline comparable to that of his drama. The large and profound relations he expressed were developed from the relatively simple dramatic method of composing with statement and counterstatement, elevated action, and burlesque. The Henry IV plays are masterpieces of the popular theater whose plays were, in Sidney's words, "neither right tragedies nor right comedies, mingling kings and clowns."

MINGLING KINGS AND CLOWNS

The fascination of Falstaff as a dramatic figure has led criticism, from Morgan's essay onward, to center *1 Henry IV* on him, and to treat the rest of the play merely as a setting for him. But despite his predominating imaginative significance, the play is centered on Prince Hal, developing in such a way as to exhibit in the prince an inclusive, sovereign nature fitted for kingship. The relation of the prince to Falstaff can be summarized fairly adequately in terms of the relation of holiday to everyday. As the nonhistorical material came to Shakespeare in *The Famous Victories of Henry the Fifth*, the prince was cast in the traditional role of the prodigal son, while his disreputable companions functioned as tempters in the same general fashion as the Vice of the morality plays. At one level Shakespeare keeps this pattern, but he shifts the emphasis away from simple moral terms. The issue, in his hands, is not whether Hal will be good or bad but whether he will be noble or degenerate, whether his holiday will become his everyday. The interregnum of a Lord of Misrule, delightful in its moment, might develop into the anarchic reign of a favorite dominating a dissolute king. Hal's secret, which he confides early to the audience, is that for him Falstaff is merely a pastime, to be dismissed in due course:

> If all the year were playing holidays,
> To sport would be as tedious as to work;
> But when they seldom come, they wish'd-for come.
> (1.2.228–30)

The prince's sports, accordingly, express not dissoluteness but a fine excess of vitality—"as full of spirit as the month of May"—together with a capacity for occasionally looking at the world as though it were upside down. His energy is controlled by an inclusive awareness of the rhythm in which he is living: despite appearances, he will not make the mistake which undid Richard II, who played at saturnalia until it caught up with him in earnest. During the battle of Shrewsbury (when, in Hotspur's phrase, "Doomsday is near"), Hal dismisses Falstaff with "What! is it a time to jest and dally now?" (5.3.57). This sense of timing, of the relation of holiday to everyday and doomsday, contributes to establishing the prince as a sovereign nature.

But the way Hal sees the relations is not the way other people see them, nor indeed the way the audience sees them until the end. The holiday-everyday antithesis is his resource for control, and in the end he makes it stick. But before that, the only clear-cut definition of relations in these terms is in his single soliloquy, after his first appearance with Falstaff. Indeed, it is remarkable how little satisfactory formulation there is of the relationships which the play explores dramatically. It is essential to the play that the prince should be misconstrued, that the king should see "riot and dishonor stain" (1.1.85) his brow, that Percy should patronize him as a "nimble-footed madcap" (4.2.95) who might easily be poisoned with a pot of ale if it were worth the trouble. But the absence of adequate summary also reflects the fact that Shakespeare was doing something which he could not summarize, which only the whole resources of his dramatic art could convey.

It is an open question, throughout *Part One*, as to just who or what Falstaff is. At the very end, when Prince John observes "This is the strangest tale that ever I heard," Hal responds with "This is the strangest fellow, brother John" (5.4.158–59). From the beginning, Falstaff is constantly renaming himself:

> Marry, then, sweet wag, when thou art king, let not us that are the squires of the night's body be called thieves of the day's beauty. Let us be Diana's Foresters, Gentlemen of the Shade, Minions of the Moon; and let men say we be men of good government.
>
> (1.2.26–31)

Here Misrule is asking to be called Good Government, as it is his role to do—though he does so with a wink which sets real good government at naught, concluding with "steal":

> men of good government, being governed as the sea is, by our noble and chase mistress the moon, under whose countenance we steal.
>
> (1.2.31–33)

I have considered [elsewhere] how the witty equivocation Falstaff practices, like that of Nashe's Bacchus and other apologists for folly and vice, alludes to the very morality it is flouting. Such "damnable iteration" is a sport that implies a rolling-eyed awareness of both sides of the moral medal; the prince summarizes it in saying that Sir John "was never yet a breaker of proverbs. He will give the devil his due" (1.2.131–33). It is also a game to be played with cards close to the chest. A Lord of Misrule naturally does not call himself Lord of Misrule in setting out to reign, but takes some title with the life of pretense in it. Falstaff's pretensions, moreover, are not limited to one occasion, for he is not properly a holiday lord, but a *de facto* buffoon who makes his way by continually seizing, catch as catch can, on what names and meanings the moment offers. He is not a professed buffoon— few buffoons, in life, are apt to be. In Renaissance courts, the role of buffoon was recognized but not necessarily formalized, not necessarily altogether distinct from the role of favorite. And he is a highwayman: Shakespeare draws on the euphemistic, mock-chivalric cant by which "the profession" grace themselves. Falstaff in *Part One* plays it that he is Hal's friend, a gentleman, a "gentleman of the shade," and a soldier; he even enjoys turning the tables with "Thou has done much harm upon me, Hal . . . I must give over this life, and I will give it over . . . I'll be damn'd for never a king's son in Christendom" (1.2.102–9). It is the essence of his character, and his role, in *Part One*, that he never comes to rest where we can see him for what he "is." He is always in motion, always adopting postures, assuming characters.

That he does indeed care for Hal can be conveyed in performance without imposing sentimental tableaux on the action, provided that actors and producer recognize that he cares for the prince after his own fashion. It is from the prince that he chiefly gets his meaning, as it is from real kings that mock kings always get their meaning. We can believe it when we hear in *Henry V* that banishment has "killed his heart" (2.1.92). But to make much of a personal affection for the prince is a misconceived way to find meaning in Falstaff. His extraordinary meaningfulness comes from the way he manages to live "out of all order, out of all compass" by his wit and his wits; and from the way he keeps reflecting on the rest of the action, at first indirectly by the mock roles that he plays, at the end directly by his comments at the battle. Through this burlesque and mockery an intelligence of the highest order is expressed. It is not always clear whether the intelligence is Falstaff's or the dramatist's; often the question need not arise. Romantic criticism went the limit in ascribing a God-like superiority to the character, to the point of insisting that he tells the lies about the multiplying men in buckram merely to amuse, that he knew all the time at Gadshill that it was with Hal and Poins that he fought. To go so far in that direction obviously destroys the drama—spoils the joke in the case of the "incomprehensible lies," a joke which, as E. E. Stoll abundantly demonstrates, must be a joke *on* Falstaff. On the other hand, I see no reason why actor and producer should not do all they can to make us enjoy the intellectual mastery involved in Falstaff's comic resource and power of humorous redefinition. It is crucial that he should not be made so superior that he is never in predicaments, for his genius is expressed in getting out of them. But he does have genius, as Maurice Morgan rightly insisted though in a misconceived way. Through his part Shakespeare expressed attitudes towards experience which, grounded in a saturnalian reversal of values, went beyond that to include a radical challenge to received ideas.

Throughout the first three acts of *Part One*, the Falstaff comedy is continuously responsive to the serious action. There are constant parallels and contrasts with what happens at court or with the rebels. And yet these parallels are not explicitly noticed; the relations are presented, not formulated. So the first scene ends in a mood of urgency, with the tired king urging hast: "come yourself with speed to us again." The second scene opens with Hal asking Falstaff "What a devil hast thou to do with the time of day?" The prose in which he explains why time is nothing to Sir John is wonderfully leisurely and abundant, an elegant sort of talk that has all the time in the world to enjoy the completion of its schematized patterns:

> Unless hours were cups of sack, and minutes capons, and clocks
> the tongues of bawds, and dials the signs of leaping houses, and
> the blessed sun himself a fair hot wench in flame-colored taffata,
> I see no reason why thou shouldst be so superfluous to demand
> the time of day.
>
> (1.2.7–13)

The same difference in the attitude towards tune runs throughout and goes with the difference between verse and prose mediums. A similar contrast obtains about lese majesty. Thus at their first appearance Falstaff insults Hal's majesty with casual, off-hand wit which the prince tolerates (while getting his own back by jibing at Falstaff's girth):

> And I prithee, sweet wag, when thou art king, as God
> save thy Grace—Majesty I should say, for grace
> thou wilt have none—
> PRINCE: What, none?
> FALSTAFF: No, by my troth; not so much as will serve
> to be prologue to an egg and butter.
> PRINCE: Well, how then? Come, roundly, roundly.
>
> (1.2.17–25)

In the next scene, we see Worcester calling into question the grace of Bolingbroke, "that same greatness to which our own hands / Have holp to make so portly" (1.3.12–13). The king's response is immediate and drastic, and his lines point a moral that Hal seems to be ignoring:

> Worcester, get thee gone; for I do see
> Danger and disobedience in thine eye.
> O, sir, your presence is too bold and peremptory,
> And majesty might never yet endure
> The moody frontier of a servant brow.
>
> (1.3.15–19)

Similar parallels run between Hotspur's heroics and Falstaff's mock-heroics. In the third scene we hear Hotspur talking of "an easy leap / To pluck bright honor from the pale-face'd moon" (1.3.201–2). Then in the robbery,

Falstaff is complaining that "Eight yards of uneven ground is threescore and ten miles afoot for me," and asking "Have you any levers to lift me up again, being down?" (2.2.25–28, 36) After Hotspur enters exclaiming against the cowardly lord who has written that he will not join the rebellion, we have Falstaff's entrance to the tune of "A plague of all cowards" (2.4.127). And so on, and so on. Shakespeare's art has reached the point where he makes everything foil to everything else. Hal's imagery, in his soliloquy, shows the dramatist thinking about such relations: "like bright metal on a sullen ground, / My reformation, glitt'ring o'er my fault" (1.2.236–37).

Now it is not true that Falstaff's impudence about Hal's grace undercuts Bolingbroke's majesty, nor that Sir John's posturing as a hero among cowards invalidates the heroic commitment Hotspur expresses when he says "but I tell you, my lord fool, out of this nettle, danger, we pluck this flower, safety" (1.3.11–12). The relationship is not one of a mocking echo. Instead, there is a certain distance between the comic and serious strains which leaves room for a complex interaction, organized by the crucial role of the prince. We are invited, by the king's unfavorable comparison in the opening scene, to see the prince in relation to Hotspur. And Hal himself, in the midst of his Boars Head revel, compares himself with Hotspur. In telling Poins of his encounter with the drawers among the hogsheads of the wine-cellar, he says "I have sounded the very bass-string of humility," goes on to note what he has gained by it, "I can drink with any tinker in his own language during my life," and concludes with "I tell thee, Ned, thou hast lost much honour that thou wert not with me in this action" (2.4.5, 20–24). His mock-heroic way of talking about "this action" shows how well he knows how to value it from a princely vantage. But the remark cuts two ways. For running the gamut of society *is* an important action: after their experiment with Francis and his "Anon, anon, sir," the prince exclaims:

> That ever this fellow should have fewer words than a parrot, and yet the son of a woman! . . . I am not yet of Percy's mind, the Hotspur of the North; he that kills me some six or seven dozen of Scots at a breakfast, washes his hands, and says to his wife, "Fie upon this quiet life! I want work." "O my sweet Harry," says she, "how many hast thou kill'd to-day?" "Give my roan horse a drench," says he, and answers "Some fourteen," an hour after, "a trifle, a trifle." I prithee call in Falstaff. I'll play Percy, and that damn'd brawn shall play Dame Mortimer his wife.
> (2.1.110–24)

It is the narrowness and obliviousness of the martial hero that Hal's mockery brings out; here his awareness explicitly spans the distance between the separate strains of the action; indeed, the distance is made the measure of the kingliness of his nature. His "I am not *yet* of Percy's mind" implies what he later promises his father (the commercial image he employs reflects his ability to use, after his father's fashion, the politician's calculation and indirection):

> Percy is but my factor, good my lord,
> To engross up glorious deeds on my behalf.
> (3.2.147–48)

In the Boars Head Tavern scene, Hal never carries out the plan of playing Percy to Falstaff's Dame Mortimer; in effect he has played both their parts already in his snatch of mimicry. But Falstaff provides him with a continuous exercise in the consciousness that comes from playing at being what one is not, and from seeing through such playing.

Even here, where one world does comment on another explicitly, Hotspur's quality is not invalidated; rather, his achievement is *placed*. It is included within a wider field which contains also the drawers, mine host, Mistress Quickly, and by implication, not only "all the good lads of Eastcheap" but all the estates of England. When we saw Hotspur and his Lady, he was not foolish, but delightful in his headlong, spontaneous way. His Lady has a certain pathos in the complaints which serve to convey how all absorbing his battle passion is. But the joke is with him as he mocks her:

> Love? I love thee not;
> I care not for thee, Kate. This is no world
> To play with mammets and to tilt with lips.
> We must have bloody noses and crack'd crowns,
> And pass them current, too. Gods me, my horse!
> (2.3.93–97)

One could make some very broad fun of Hotspur's preference for his horse over his wife. But there is nothing of the kind in Shakespeare: here and later, his treatment values the conversion of love into war as one of the important human powers. Hotspur has the fullness of life and the unforced integrity of the great aristocrat who has never known what it is to cramp his own style. His style shows it; he speaks the richest, freshest poetry of the play, in lines that take all the scope they need to fulfill feeling and perception:

> oft the teeming earth
> Is with a kind of colic pinch'd and vex'd
> By the imprisoning of unruly wind
> Within her womb, which, for enlargement striving,
> Shakes the old beldame earth and topples down
> Steeples and mossgrown towers. At your birth
> Our grandam earth, having this distemp'rature,
> In passion shook.
>   GLENDOWER: Cousin, of many men
> I do not bear these crossings. Give me leave
> To tell you once again that at my birth
> The front of heaven was full of fiery shapes,
> The goats ran from the mountains, and the herds
> Were strangely clamorous to the frighted fields.
>
>   (3.1.28 – 40)

The established life of moss-grown towers is in Percy's poetic speech, as the grazed-over Welsh mountains are in Glendower's. They are both strong; everybody in this play is strong in his own way. Hotspur's humor is untrammeled, like his verse, based on the heedless empiricism of an active, secure nobleman:

> GLENDOWER: I can call spirits from the vasty deep.
> HOTSPUR: Why, so can I, or so can any man;
> But will they come when you do call for them?
>
>   (3.1.53 –55)

His unconsciousness makes him, at other moments. a comic if winning figure, as the limitations of his feudal virtues are brought out: his want of tact and judgment, his choleric man's forgetfulness, his sudden boyish habit of leaping to conclusions, the noble but also comical way he can be carried away by "imagination of some great exploit" (1.3.199), or by indignation at "this vile politician, Bolingbroke" (1.3.241). Professor Lily B. Campbell has demonstrated that the rebellion of the Northern Earls in 1570 was present for Shakespeare's audience in watching the Percy family in the play. The remoteness of this rough north country life from the London world of his audience, as well as its aristocratic charm, are conveyed when Hotspur tell his wife that she swears "like a comfit-maker's wife,"

> As if thou ne'er walk'st further than Finsbury.
> Swear me, Kate, like a lady as thou art,
> A good mouth-filling oath; and leave 'in sooth'

> And such protest of pepper gingerbread
> To velvet guards and Sunday citizens
> (3.1.255–59)

It is the various strengths of a stirring world, not deficiencies, which make the conflict in *1 Henry IV*. Even the humble carriers, and the professional, thieves are full of themselves and their business:

> I am joined with no foot land-rakers, no long-staff sixpenny strikers, none of these mad mustachio purple-hued maltworms; but with nobility and tranquillity, burgomasters and great oneyers, such as can hold in, such as will strike sooner than speak, and speak sooner than drink, and drink sooner than pray; and yet, zounds, I lie; for they pray continually to their saint, the commonwealth, or rather, not pray to her, but prey on her, for they ride up and down on her and make her their boots.
> (2.1.81–91)

In his early history play, *2 Henry IV*, as we have noticed, Shakespeare used his clowns to present the Jack Cade rebellion as a saturnalia ignorantly undertaken in earnest, a highly-stylized piece of dramaturgy, which he brings off triumphantly. In this more complex play the underworld is presented as endemic disorder alongside the crisis of noble rebellion: the king's lines are apposite when he says that insurrection can always mobilize

> moody beggars, starving for a time
> Of pell-mell havoc and confusion
> (5.1.81–82)

Falstaff places himself in saying "Well, God be thanked for these rebels. They offend none but the virtuous. I laud them, I praise them."

The whole effect, in the opening acts, when there is little commentary on the spectacle as a whole, is of life overflowing its bounds by sheer vitality. Thieves and rebels and honest men—"one that hath abundance of charge too, God knows what" (2.1.64)—ride up and down on the commonwealth, pray to her and prey on her. Hotspur exults that "That roan shall be my throne" (2.3.73). Falstaff exclaims, "Shall I? Content. This chair shall be my state" (2.4.415). Hal summarizes the effect, after Hotspur is dead, with

> When that this body did contain a spirit,
> A kingdom for it was too small a bound.
> (5.4.89–90)

The stillness when he says this, at the close of the battle, is the moment when his royalty is made manifest. When he stands poised above the prostrate bodies of Hotspur and Falstaff, his position on the stage and his lines about the two heroes express a nature which includes within a larger order the now subordinated parts of life which are represented in those two: in Hotspur, honor, the social obligation to courage and self-sacrifice, a value which has been isolated in this magnificently anarchical feudal lord to become almost everything; and in Falstaff, the complementary *joie de vivre* which rejects all social obligations with "I like not such grinning honour as Sir Walter hath. Give me life" (5.3.61).

GETTING RID OF BAD LUCK BY COMEDY

But Falstaff does not stay dead. He jumps up in a triumph which, like Bottom coming alive after Pyramus is dead, reminds one of the comic resurrections in the St. George plays. He comes back to life because he is still relevant. His apology for counterfeiting cuts deeply indeed, because it does not apply merely to himself; we can relate it, as William Empson has shown, to the counterfeiting of the king. Bolingbroke too knows when it is time to counterfeit, both in this battle, where he survives because he has many marching in his coats, and throughout a political career where, as he acknowledges to Hal, he manipulates the symbols of majesty with a calculating concern for ulterior results. L. C. Knights, noticing this relation and the burlesque, elsewhere in Falstaff's part, of the attitudes of chivalry, concluded with nineteenth-century critics like Ulrici and Victor Hugo that the comedy should be taken as a devastating satire on war and government. But this is obviously an impossible, anachronistic view, based on the assumption of the age of individualism that politics and war are unnatural activities that can be done without. Mr. Knights would have it that the audience would feel a jeering response when Henry sonorously declares, after Shrewsbury: "Thus ever did rebellion find rebuke." This interpretation makes a shambles of the heroic moments of the play—makes them clearly impossible to act. My own view, as will be clear, is that the dynamic relation of comedy and serious action is saturnalian rather than satiric, that the misrule works, through the whole dramatic rhythm, to consolidate rule. But it is also true, as Mr. Empson remarks, that "the double plot is carrying a fearful strain here." Shakespeare is putting an enormous pressure on the comedy to resolve the challenge posed by the ironic perceptions presented in his historical action.

The process at work, here and earlier in the play, can be made clearer,

I hope, by reference now to the carrying off of bad luck by the scapegoat of saturnalian ritual. We do not need to assume that Shakespeare had any such ritual patterns consciously in mind; whatever his conscious intention, it seems to me that these analogues illuminate patterns which his poetic drama presents concretely and dramatically. After such figures as the Mardi Gras or Carnival have presided over a revel, they are frequently turned on by their followers, tried in some sort of court, convicted of sins notorious in the village during the last year, and burned or buried in effigy to signify a new start. In other ceremonies described in *The Golden Bough*, mockery kings appear as recognizable substitutes for real kings, stand trial in their stead, and carry away the evils of their realms into exile or death. One such scapegoat figure, as remote historically as could be from Shakespeare, is the Tibetan King of the Years, who enjoyed ten days' misrule during the annual holiday of Buddhist monks at Lhasa. At the climax of his ceremony, after doing what he liked while collecting bad luck by shaking a black yak's tail over the people, he mounted the temple steps and ridiculed the representative of the Grand Llama, proclaiming heresies like "What we perceive through the five senses is no illusion. All you teach is untrue." A few minutes later, discredited by a cast of loaded dice, he was chased off to exile and possible death in the mountains. One cannot help thinking of Falstaff's catechism on honor, spoken just before another valuation of honor is expressed in the elevated blank verse of a hero confronting death: "Can honour . . . take away the grief of a wound? No . . . What is honour? a word. What is that word, honour? Air." Hal's final expulsion of Falstaff appears in the light of these analogies to carry out an impersonal pattern, not merely political but ritual in character. After the guilty reign of Bolingbroke, the prince is making a fresh start as the new king. At a level beneath the moral notions of a personal reform, we can see a nonlogical process of purification by sacrifice—the sacrifice of Falstaff. The career of the old king, a successful usurper whose conduct of affairs has been sceptical and opportunistic, has cast doubt on the validity of the whole conception of a divinely-ordained and chivalrous kingship to which Shakespeare and his society were committed. And before Bolingbroke, Richard II had given occasion for doubts about the rituals of kingship in an opposite way, by trying to use them magically. Shakespeare had shown Richard assuming that the symbols of majesty should be absolutes, that the names of legitimate power should be transcendentally effective regardless of social forces. Now both these attitudes have been projected also in Falstaff; he carries to comically delightful and degraded extremes both a magical use of moral sanctions and the complementary opportunistic manipulation and scepticism.

So the ritual analogy suggests that by turning on Falstaff as a scapegoat, as the villagers turned on their Mardi Gras, the prince can free himself from the sins, the "bad luck," of Richard's reign and of his father's reign, to become a king in whom chivalry and a sense of divine ordination are restored.

But this process of carrying off bad luck, if it is to be made *dramatically* cogent, as a symbolic action accomplished in and by dramatic form, cannot take place magically in Shakespeare's play. When it happens magically in the play, we have, I think, a failure to transform ritual into comedy. In dealing with fully successful comedy, the magical analogy is only a useful way of organizing our awareness of a complex symbolic action. The expulsion of evil works as dramatic form only in so far as it is realized in a movement from participation to rejection which happens, moment by moment, in our response to Falstaff's clowning misrule. We watch Falstaff adopt one posture after another, in the effort to give himself meaning at no cost; and moment by moment we see that the meaning is specious. So our participation is repeatedly diverted to laughter. The laughter, disbursing energy originally mobilized to respond to a valid meaning, signalizes our mastery by understanding of the tendency which had been misapplied or carried to an extreme.

Consider, for example, the use of magical notions of royal power in the most famous of all Falstaff's burlesques:

> By the Lord, I knew ye as well as he that made ye. . . . Was it for me to kill the heir apparent? Should I turn upon the true prince? Why, thou knowest I am as valiant as Hercules; but beware instinct. The lion will not touch the true prince. Instinct is a great matter. I was now a coward on instinct. I shall think the better of myself, and thee, during my life—I for a valiant lion, and thou for a true prince. But, by the Lord, lads, I am glad you have the money. Hostess, clap to the doors: watch to-night, pray to-morrow.
>
> (2.4.295–306)

Here Falstaff has recourse to the brave conception that legitimate kingship has a magical potency. This is the sort of absolutist appeal to sanctions which Richard II keeps falling back on in his desperate "conjuration" (*R.II* 3.2.23) by hyperbole:

> So when this thief, this traitor, Bolingbroke, . . .
> Shall see us rising in our throne, the East,

> His treasons will sit blushing in his face,
> Not able to endure the sight of day . . .
> The breath of worldly men cannot depose
> The deputy elected by the Lord.
> For every man that Bolingbroke hath press'd
> To lift shrewd steel against our golden crown,
> God for his Richard hath in heavenly pay
> A glorious angel.
>
> (*R.II* 3.2.47–61)

In Richard's case, a tragic irony enforces the fact that heavenly angels are of no avail if one's coffers are empty of golden angels and the Welsh army have dispersed. In Falstaff's case, the irony is comically obvious, the "lies are like the father that begets them; gross as a mountain, open, palpable" (2.4.249–50). Hal stands for the judgment side of our response, while Falstaff embodies the enthusiastic, irrepressible conviction of fantasy's omnipotence. The prince keeps returning to Falstaff's bogus "instinct"; "Now, sirs . . . You are lions too, you ran away upon instinct, you will not touch the true prince; no—fie!" (2.4.29–34). After enjoying the experience of seeing through such notions of magical majesty, he is never apt to make the mistake of assuming that, just because he is king, lions like Northumberland will not touch him. King Richard's bad luck came precisely from such an assumption—unexamined, of course, as fatal assumptions always are. Freud's account of bad luck, in *The Psychopathology of Everyday Life*, sees it as the expression of unconscious motives which resist the conscious goals of the personality. This view helps to explain how the acting out of disruptive motives in saturnalia or in comedy can serve to master potential aberration by revaluing it in relation to the whole of experience. So Falstaff, in acting out this absolutist aberration, is taking away what might have been Hal's bad luck, taking it away not in a magical way, but by extending the sphere of conscious control. The comedy is a civilized equivalent of the primitive rite. A similar mastery of potential aberration is promoted by the experience of seeing through Falstaff's burlesque of the sort of headlong chivalry presented seriously in Hotspur.

In order to put the symbolic action of the comedy in larger perspective, it will be worthwhile to consider further, for a moment, the relation of language to stage action and dramatic situation in *Richard II*. That play is a pioneering exploration of the semantics of royalty, shot through with talk about the potency and impotence of language. In the first part, we see a Richard who is possessor of an apparently magical omnipotence: for example, when he commutes Bolingbroke's banishment from ten to six years, Bolingbroke exclaims:

> How long a time lies in one little word!
> Four lagging winters and four wanton springs
> End in a word: such is the breath of kings.
>
> (R.II 1.3.213–15)

Richard assumes he has such magic breath inevitably, regardless of "the breath of worldly men." When he shouts things like "Is not the king's name twenty thousand names? / Arm, arm, my name!" he carries the absolutist assumption to the giddiest verge of absurdity. When we analyze the magical substitution of words for things in such lines, looking at them from outside the rhythm of feeling in which they occur, it seems scarcely plausible that a drama should be built around the impulse to adopt such an assumption. It seem especially implausible in our own age, when we are so conscious, on an abstract level, of the dependence of verbal efficacy on the social group. The analytical situation involves a misleading perspective, however; for, whatever your assumptions about semantics, when you have to *act*, to *be* somebody or become somebody, there is a moment when you have to have faith that the unknown world beyond will respond to the names you commit yourself to as right names. The Elizabethan mind, moreover, generally assumed that one played one's part in a divinely ordained pageant where each man *was* his name and the role his name implied. The expression of this faith, and of the outrage of it, is particularly drastic in the Elizabethan drama, which can be regarded, from this vantage, as an art form developed to express the shock and exhilaration of the discovery that life is not pageantry. As Professor Tillyard has pointed out, *Richard II* is the most ceremonial of all Shakespeare's plays, and the ceremony all comes to nothing. In Richard's deposition scene, one way in which anguish at his fall is expressed is by a focus of his loss of names: he responds to Northumberland's "My Lord—" by flinging out

> No lord of thine, thou haught insulting man,
> Nor no man's lord. I have no name, no title—
> No, not that name was given me at the font—
> But 'tis usurp'd. Alack the heavy day,
> That I have worn so many winters out
> And know not now what name to call myself!
> O that I were a mockery king of snow,
> Standing before the sun of Bolingbroke
> To melt myself away in water-drops!
>
> (R.II 4.1.253–62)

His next move is to call for the looking glass in which he stares at this face to look for the meaning the face has lost. To lose one's meaning, one's social role, is to be reduced to mere body.

Here again the tragedy can be used to illuminate the comedy. Since the Elizabethan drama was a double medium of words and of physical gestures, it frequently expressed the pathos of the loss of meaning by emphasizing moments when word and gesture, name and body, no longer go together, just as it presented the excitement of a gain of meaning by showing a body seizing on names when a hero creates his identity. In the deposition scene, Richard says "mark me how I will undo myself" (4.1.203). Then he gives away by physical gestures the symbolic meanings which have constituted that self. When at last he has no name, the anguish is that the face, the body, remain when the meaning is gone. There is also something in Richard's lines which, beneath the surface of his self-pity, relishes such undoing, a self-love which looks towards fulfillment in that final reduction of all to the body which is death. This narcissistic need for the physical is the other side of the attitude that the magic of the crown should altogether transcend the physical—and the human:

> Cover your heads, and mock not flesh and blood
> With solemn reverence. Throw away respect,
> Tradition, form, and ceremonious duty;
> For you have but mistook me all this while.
> I live with bread like you, feel want, taste grief,
> Need friends. Subjected thus,
> How can you say to me I am a king?
>   (*R.II* 3.2.171–77)

In expressing the disappointment of Richard's magical expectations, as well as their sweeping magnificence, the lines make manifest the aberration which is mastered in the play by tragic form.

The same sort of impulse is expressed and mastered by comic form in the Henry IV comedy. When Richard wishes he were a mockery king of snow, to melt before the sun of Bolingbroke, the image expresses on one side the wish to escape from the body with which he is left when his meaning is gone—to weep himself away in water drops. But the lines also look wistfully towards games of mock royalty where, since the whole thing is based on snow, the collapse of meaning need not hurt. Falstaff is such a mockery king. To be sure, he is flesh and blood, of a kind: he is tallow, anyway. He "sweats to death / And lards the lean earth as he walks along." Of course he is not just a mockery, not just his role, not just bombast. Shakespeare, as always, makes the symbolic role the product of a life which includes contradictions of it, such as the morning-after regrets when Falstaff thinks of the inside of a church and notices that his skin hangs about him like an old lady's loose gown. Falstaff is human enough so that "Were't not for laughing . . . [we]should pity him." But we do laugh, because when Falstaff's meanings collapse, little but make-believe has been lost:

> PRINCE: Thy state is taken for a join'd-stool, thy golden
>   sceptre for a leaden dagger, and thy precious rich crown
>   for a pitiful bald crown.
>
> (2.4.418–20)

Falstaff's effort to make his body and furnishings mean sovereignty is doomed from the start; he must work with a leaden dagger, the equivalent of a Vice's dagger of lath. But Falstaff does have golden words, and an inexhaustible vitality in using them. He can name himself nobly, reordering the world by words so as to do himself credit:

> No, my good lord. Banish Peto, banish Bardolph, banish Poins; but for sweet Jack Falstaff, kind Jack Falstaff, true Jack Falstaff, valiant Jack Falstaff, and therefore more valiant being, as he is, old Jack Falstaff, banish not him thy Harry's company, banish not him thy Harry's company. Banish plump Jack, and banish all the world!
>
> (2.4.519–27)

I quote such familiar lines to recall their effect of incantation: they embody an effort at a kind of magical naming. Each repetition of "sweet Jack Falstaff, kind Jack Falstaff" aggrandizes an identity which the serial clauses caress and cherish. At the very end, in "plump Jack," the disreputable belly is glorified.

In valid heroic and majestic action, the bodies of the personages are constantly being elevated by becoming the vehicles of social meanings; in the comedy, such elevation becomes burlesque, and in the repeated failures to achieve a fusion of body and symbol, abstract meanings keep falling back into the physical. "A plague of sighing and grief! it blows a man up like a bladder" (2.4.365–66). The repetition of such joking about Falstaff's belly makes it meaningful in a very special way, as a symbol of the process of inflation and collapse of meaning. So it represents the power of the individual life to continue despite the collapse of social roles. This continuing on beyond definitions is after all what we call "the body" in one main meaning of the term: Falstaff's belly is thus the essence of body—an essence which can be defined only dynamically, by failures of meaning. The effect of indestructible vitality is reinforced by the association of Falstaff's figure with the gay eating and drinking of Shrove Tuesday and Carnival. Whereas, in the tragedy, the reduction is to a body which can only die, here reduction is to a body which typifies our power to eat and drink our way through a shambles of intellectual and moral contradictions.

So we cannot resist sharing Falstaff's genial self-love when he commends his vision of plump Jack to the prince, just as we share the ingenuous self-love of a little child. But the dramatist is ever on the alert to enforce the ironies that dog the tendency of fantasy to equate the self with "all the world." So a most monstrous watch comes beating at the doors which have been clapped to against care; everyday breaks in on holiday.

The Growth of Hal

Ricardo J. Quinones

The shadow of Richard II hangs over the waywardness of Hal in *1 Henry IV*. The young prince is threatened with the same historical isolation and discontinuity. In their critical confrontation, his father the King accuses him of straying "quite from the light of all thy ancestors." His place on the council has been "rudely lost" to his younger brother. "The hope and expectation of thy time / Is ruined." He then startles his son's self-possession by declaring that Percy is more like his true heir, and that he (Hal) is more like Richard.

> [Percy] hath more worldly interest to the state
> Than thou, the shadow of succession.
>
> (3.2.98–99)

To be sure, the scope of Hal's conversion can be exaggerated. As we insisted [elsewhere] with Petrarch and Montaigne, before one can be reformed there must be some prior inclination to reformation: something convertible must inhere before conversion. And Hal's first soliloquy where he shows some of his father's calculation and vows to redeem his time, can be taken to show that the ground was ready. Yet there is a difference between vowing to do something, knowing that one will, and actually doing it. There is something headstrong and, in a way, deceived in that young man who knows his capacities and yet feels no need to demonstrate them to other people. This is no mean alteration; it can be summarized in

---

From *The Renaissance Discovery of Time.* © 1972 by the President and Fellows of Harvard College. Harvard University Press, 1972.

the change from adolescence to adulthood. The father is crucial in this transformation as is the son's personal pride, his felt need to redeem his time to fulfill his "hopes and expectations." As we have seen in Dante and Petrarch, both of these elements, the father-figure (in Hal's case, his actual father) and a sense of time, are crucial in this phase of commitment. The argument of time, in its ramifications, is the instrument of conversion from the aesthetic to the ethical stage of existence.

Kierkegaard's terminology is highly useful in describing Shakespeare's character delineation. In Dante and Petrarch the aesthetic stage importantly includes a reliance on the substitute satisfactions of art and beauty. But in each it extends somewhat beyond that to the aesthetic personality. In the *Purgatorio* Dante had to change his interest as he ceased to be a passive witness and began to take more positive action. Petrarch's aesthetic stage had even more to do with a preference for contemplative distance and consciousness rather than commitment and moral effort. Although Shakespeare's characters have something of the "literary" in them (Richard II and the "bookish" Henry IV), they fulfill the aesthetic function more in terms of personality. What strictly joins Hal with Richard II (and through him with other representatives of the aesthetic—although at the time we did not so designate them—Marlowe's Calyphas in *II Tamburlaine*, Edward II, and Dr. Faustus) is (1) the inclination to be a spectator rather than an actor, (2) a divorce between consciousness and willed action, and (3) a kind of identity-diffusion. Not all of these figures fully enjoy all three characteristics, but all have a sufficient share of them to invalidate their effectiveness in the temporal realm. It is to spare his son their fates (particularly that of Richard II) that the concerned father puts before Hal an objective picture of his actions—the way his behavior is read by both the public and his father.

The structure of *1* and *2 Henry IV*—the multiple plot levels—is essential to the character of Hal. This technical device (also employed in *A Midsummer Night's Dream*) was of major usefulness to Shakespeare from the mid-nineties on. If in *Henry IV* he has found his character and his theme, in the multiple plot he has found the mechanism for revealing them. Richard II too, has multiple personalities, but they are all imaginary, and he only gives flight to them when the hard world of history presents him with the truth of his nothingness. But Hal still has time, and with time, choice. Hal is a fluid participant in multiple levels of existence. In many ways that is his glory and, as we shall see, his redemption. But it can also be his destruction if he refuses to commit himself to a single identity, and if he refuses to accept the responsibilities and historical limitations into which he was born. We come here again to a basic characteristic and function of time in the Renaissance and its relationship with the possibilities of variety. Petrarch, too, accused himself of distraction, of having too many options, and thus neglecting the most important condition of his soul. Time was a crucial element in his conversion. Later in the Renaissance, in Alberti's *regola*, we saw the rationale for scheduling. Each morning he charted the things to be done that day, and assigned a time to them. In this way the variety of his interests did not prove his undoing, and all things were accomplished *con ordine*. In Guarino, too, we observed an explicit connection between scheduling and variety. "So many subjects claim our attention that concentration and thoroughness are impossible" unless we regulate our existence. And the education of Gargantua is a greater dramatic example of the arrangement of time required to order many interests. Although there is no odor of schedule in Hal, still time is about its same purpose as in these other Renaissance writers: it channels and makes more effective, it marshalls into a functioning unity, the variety of interests and talents that otherwise might be merely dissipated, and to their possessor's harm.

This quality in his prince attests also to Shakespeare's talent for comprehensiveness, his ability to recreate imaginatively various levels of existence. It further shows his concern with the many ways of regarding reality, with consciousness trying to feel out and determine the nature of the world. Yet while this multifaceted world reveals a rich Renaissance sense of variety and possibility, and is related to the artist's own protean capacities, Shakespeare fully recognized the dangers involved. Not only are potentially ideal characters threatened or destroyed by a dissipation of energy, but Shakespeare's evil characters also seem unsettled and chameleon-like:

> Why, I can smile, and murther whiles I smile,
> And cry "Content!" to that which grieves my heart.
> And wet my cheeks with artificial tears,
> And frame my face to all occasions:
>
> . . . .
>
> I can add colours to the chameleon,
> Change shapes with Proteus for advantages,
> And set the murderous Machiavel to school.
> (*3 Henry VI* 3.2.182–85, 191–93)

We must remember that Iago, too, was "motiveless" in his malignity. The mind is a dangerous and shifting place, "no-man fathomed." And while Romantic critics like Bradley and Yeats groaned at the heavy ethic of Lancaster, there is every indication that their "strong fixed" house, "like a mountain" lent some stability to a world that for Shakespeare was becoming increasingly complex. Their world of time and consequence might bear too great a yoke (although we must remember that Hal's own modified comprehensiveness represented a more graceful advance on that "silent king" his father), yet it was preferable to the uncontrolled actor Richard III and to the vainly deluded and destroyed Henry VI and Richard II.

In discussing the argument of time it is relevant to mention a very consistent factor in the "weak king" type that Hal must transcend. *Edward II* opens with Gaveston reading a letter telling him of the death of the king's father. *Henry VI* begins with the inauspicious funeral procession of his father. Richard II, too, was a child king, who warred on his father's house. Dr. Faustus, with infinite possibilities before him, came from parents "base of stock" and consequently in no position to give him guidance. And what must assume some significance, given these other details, the young man of the sonnets is without a father. Sonnet 3 refers to his mother in the present tense, as still living, while sonnet 13 distinctly refers to his father in the past tense—"You had a father—let your son say so." The absence of Northumberland in Hotspur's defeat is thus crucial. The office of the father is to educate the will, to deflate the "swoll'n cunning of self-conceit"—to strip the young man of vain illusions of permanence and omnipotence. He stands for an external objective world that is threatening to any deluded vanity. As such the father embodies the sense of time, and we are justified, I believe, in recalling the role of Cato in Dante's temporal *cantica*, the *Purgatorio*, and that of Augustine in Petrarch's *Secretum*.

That Hal required the important interview with his father in the very center of *1 Henry IV*, even after his seemingly self-assured soliloquy, is proved by the fact that the intervening scenes all show him as an uninvolved participant in actions where the play element is strong and where he believes that his real self is essentially untouched by his involvements. To justify the Gadshill episode, he declares, "Once in my days I'll be a madcap," (1.2.160). He is in rollicking humor as he tells of the drinking buddies he has just encountered, and will play with Francis, the rather limited waiter, "to drive away the time till Falstaff come" (2.4.31). he is "now of all humours that have showed themselves humours since the old days of good-man Adam to the pupil age of this present twelve o'clock at midnight" (1.4–7). He is not of Percy's mind, "I prithee call in Falstaff. I'll play Percy" (122).

And after the jest of catching Falstaff in his "incomprehensible lies," he yields to the gaiety of the moment and Falstaff's urging, "Shall we have a play extempore?" (308). But the outside world intrudes on this play world.

Sir John Bracy brings news of the Percy uprising, yet Hal takes it all lightly. And at the prospect of a chiding from his father the next day, he agrees with Falstaff's suggestion to play out the scene: "If thou love me, practice an answer" (411). This action, while ostensibly comic, reveals some serious motives: Falstaff's insistent defense of himself, and the prince's suddenly serious vow of banishment "I do, I will" (628). But this scene also is interrupted—this time by the knocking of the sheriff's men. Falstaff urges, "Play out the play. I have much to say in the behalf of that Falstaff" (531). The prince covers for him, one of several crucial scenes in the play where he pays the bill and spares Falstaff a reckoning. Despite all the wonderful fun and humor of the prince, it is obvious that here he is a different individual from the one who emerges following the interview with his father.

Several other elements in the father's lecture to his son remain important. We get some notion of what is means to redeem the time, when the king declares what he would have been if, at their relative stages, he had been like Hal, "so stale and cheap to vulgar company." The opinion of the people would have still remained loyal to Richard,

> And left me in reputeless banishment,
> A fellow of no mark nor likelihood.
> (3.2.44–45)

To be a "somebody," to have a name, is crucial in Shakespeare's historical argument of time. (How much young Bolingbroke's sense of identity, "Harry of Hereford, Lancaster, and Derby / Am I" contrasts with Richard's subsequent namelessness and nothingness.) And to achieve this status one must learn the importance of "appearances" and the necessity of manipulating the human mechanism. That is how Bolingbroke came to be king, while

> The skipping King, he ambled up and down
> With shallow jesters and rash bavin wits,
> Soon kindled and soon burnt.
> (60–62)

An interesting element in the House of Lancaster is the way the son will repeat the attitudes and even the words of the father. "Soon kindled and soon burnt" recalls the fate old John of Gaunt predicted for Richard's "light vanity," which "consuming means, soon preys upon itself." There is a fundamental seriousness in the House of Lancaster that has only scorn for the ineffective bursts of wit and fancy that play themselves out and produce nothing of solid and enduring reality. Hal, too, will be in a position to reject "light vanity."

But at the moment, his antagonist Hotspur is the occasion that informs against him. How irritating it is for the son to hear invidious comparisons with a more successful coeval. It is of course to emphasize this rivalrous competition and their destined confrontation and to increase the sting of the comparison that Shakespeare transforms the ages of Hal and Hotspur, making them contemporaries, when, in historical fact, Hotspur was older than Henry IV. But Hotspur is now Hal's Fortinbras. And to his father's lavish praise of "this Hotspur, Mars in swathling clothes" and to the suggestion that Hal would more likely fight in Percy's hire through fear and his patent inclination toward lowness, Hal's native pride stiffens

> Do not think so. You shall not find it so.
> And God forgive them that so much have sway'd
> Your majesty's good thoughts away from me.
> I will redeem all this on Percy's head
> And, in the closing of some glorious day,
> Be bold to tell you that I am your son.
>
> (129–34)

Despite the sunny avowal, the language of economics persists. Percy is but his factor,

> And I will call him to so strict account
> That he shall render every glory up,
> Yea, even the slightest worship of his time,
> Or I will tear the reckoning from his heart.
>
> (147–52)

In tracing the fortunes of Hal in *Parts One* and *Two*, one is indeed surprised to learn that after his splendid reformation he must again prove himself to his father. Yet the tone of *Part Two* has become so sombre, so intensified, and so dark, with such new problems raised, that one does not object to the replay. However much it may have been an afterthought, *Part Two* is radically different in atmosphere. The gaiety and the sun-drenched possibilities of *Part One* are weighted down by sickness, guilt, and the apparently unending troubles of Henry IV's reign. Falstaff's age and melancholy are more apparent; when we first meet him he is desperately in need of money. Hal himself is wearied with his former friends. At a crucial point of father-son feeling, Hal's cronies cross his true sentiments and make it appear that Hal would only be a hypocrite were he to show sadness at this father's illness: "By this hand, thou thinkest me as far in the devil's book as thou and Falstaff for obduracy and persistency. Let the end try the man. But I tell thee, my heart bleeds inwardly that my father is so sick; and keeping such vile company as thou art hath in reason taken from me all ostentation of sorrow" (2.2.48–54). His father had warned him of "vile participation," and Hal comes now to experience it in his own way.

Time is no longer altogether in front of Hal. He begins to feel the weight of his own waste. Here, by focusing on some elements of the argument of time, we can perceive a dramatic justification of *Part Two*. As in all father-son encounters, the older voice tries to persuade the younger person of a truth that he did not learn abstractly himself, but rather gained from experience. The absence of the same experience in the son and the importance of the lesson account for the mounting exasperation and impatience in the father. It is not until the son himself knows by experience the lessons of time—and this lesson all too often is only learned, unfortunately, in the shadow of the father's death—that he comes to appreciate in his own marrow the truths that previously were mere abstractions. We have seen this already in the dynamic of Petrarch's development. It was only by experience that the lessons of time could be really learned, and a true conversion take place. The advance of *Part Two* over its predecessor is precisely here. In *Part One* Hal was still glorious; in *Part Two*, he begins to feel the waste of his own energies and talents. Falstaff's overweening letter tells the prince that Poins has been speaking of a marriage between his sister and Hal. When Hal asks if this is true, Poins in effect declares that he could do worse. These involvements depress the prince: "Well, thus we play the fools with the time, and the spirits of the wise sit in the clouds and mock us" (2.2.154–57). Yet he undertakes one more jest to catch Falstaff. Hiding behind the arras he has the opportunity to observe "desire outlive performance." And although Falstaff, as in *Part One*, wriggles out of the trap, the scene ends disappointingly. News of war again intrudes, but this time only serves to burden the prince with guilt:

> By heaven, Poins, I feel me much to blame
> So idly to profane the precious time,
> When tempest of commotion, like the South,
> Borne with black vapour, doth begin to melt
> And drop upon our bare unarmed heads.
>
> (2.4.390–94)

So, too, the king's burden is heavier in *Part Two*. The end of his life is approaching and the crucial action of his life is still unjustified. The source of concern is his as yet unredeemed son. Through Hal's dereliction the king sees his own guilt reflected. Rather than an event leading to a better future, his accession to the throne seems only to be a curse. Should Henry IV provide an orderly succession, the ambiguities surrounding his rise to power would be resolved. The doubtful resolution of the prince turns back on Bolingbroke. In *Richard II* he is already aware that "if any plague hang over us, 'tis he." And in *Part One*, his first words to his son emphasize this fear that Henry is Henry's punishment:

> I know not whether God will have it so,
> For some displeasing service I have done,
> That, in his secret doom, out of my blood
> He'll breed revengement and a scourge for me;
> But thou dost in thy passages of life
> Make me believe that thou are only mark'd
> For the hot vengeance and the rod of heaven
> To punish my mistreadings.
>
> (3.2.4–11)

In *Part Two* (3.1), the worn and sleepless king has time to reflect on the ironies of history. Ten years ago Richard and Northumberland were friends; eight years ago he and Percy were friends. Rather than simple "revolution of the times," a formal line, reminiscent of the curses of the first tetralogy, is given these events by Richard's prediction of them. To a certain point, then, the issues of the first and second tetralogy follow similar courses. Action in the first merely brings on further action; a curse seems to operate over the whole. In the second, as far as Henry IV is aware, the same is true. His act of revolution seems to have involved him in a series of necessary actions that hold not promise for resolution. His hope in the time to come is also blighted by his son. Not only has Hal, as we have seen, turned the garden of his youth in to a weedy patch, and thus reversed one benevolent process in generation, he threatens the more public hopes of the king:

> The blood weeps from my heart when I do shape,
> In forms imaginary, th' unguided days
> And rotten times that you shall look upon
> When I am sleeping with my ancestors.
>
> (4.4.54–61)

This same double curse that produces bitter emulation within the family and disorder in society is the object of the king's attack on his son in their moving interview in *Part Two*. "See, sons, what things you are . . ."

(4.5.65ff.). Believing that Hal seized the crown before his death, Henry IV assails this ingratitude:

> For this the foolish over-careful fathers
> Have broke their sleep with thoughts, their brains with care,
> Their bones with industry:
>
> . . . .
>
> When like the bee tolling from every flower
> The virtuous sweets,
> Our thighs pack'd with wax, our mouths with honey,
> We bring it to the hive, and, like the bees,
> Are murd'red for our pains. This bitter taste
> Yields his engrossments to the ending father.

That his son will dance on his grave, is the fear—perhaps ages old—that the anguished father expresses. His sense of injury at the apparent ingratitude is strong, "Canst thou not forbear me half an hour?" As in *Tamburlaine*, but without that play's zesty endorsement, the universe becomes an arena of naturalistic place-taking from which no service or relationship is immune. Henry IV, so the curse would run, who usurped the position of Richard II, is driven from office by his son. This is the way of the universe, where no channels exist that offer protection against the currents of emulation. The dilemma of Henry IV is precisely here: although he came to the crown through ambiguous means, he hopes to establish an orderly and a clear succession. His war is preeminently with an original sin, which his son's behavior seems to confirm. Yet his concern extends beyond his personal situation to the national consequences that his distraught fears imagine:

> O my poor kingdom, sick with civil blows!
> When that my care would not withhold thy riots,
> What wilt thou do when riot is thy care?
> O, thou wilt be a wilderness again,
> Peopled with wolves, thy old inhabitants!
>
> (134–38)

It is part of Shakespeare's eminent reasonableness, of course, that the accusing father is wrong in his opinion of his son. But the concern is genuine, and it is this concern which turns out to be an expiating factor, in the second tetralogy, in the validation of the House of Lancaster. The two tetralogies assume a fundamental relationship with the *Oresteia*, where similarly two basic acts are performed, one vindicated, the other not. The House of York in the first tetralogy was unable to muster valid principles to justify its revolution. Yorkist vision, consumed by the golden crown, rarely rose to larger perspectives of time and place; its motives proved to result in a root individualism that in turn devours York's own house, "I am myself alone." It is precisely this vision of life that Henry IV, however tainted he might be, criticizes in his own son. The Yorkists are like Clytemnestra, who brazenly exults over the fallen husband. Her own impure motives reveal themselves in the way her kingdom grinds to a dead stop, in the horror of fear and nightmare. On Orestes, however, a necessity operates that compells him toward the horrendous deed, and his own righteousness is revealed in the guilt that he feels, and by the pilgrimage of expiation he must undergo. His conscience has not been brazened by the act. Like Henry IV, his very guilt is part of the breaking of the curse.

This is especially so, to return to Shakespeare's second tetralogy, when the father's guilt is centered on Hal and his tenure, on the kind of king he will be. In one of his denunciations of his son, Henry IV charges that his attitude toward government is frivolous: "O foolish youth! / Thou seek'st the greatness that will overwhelm thee" (2 Henry IV 4.5.96–97). Yet it is precisely in his sense of the burdens of rule and the other difficulties and either/or necessities of the world of time that Henry most duplicates his father. Unlike the Yorkists' frequent apostrophes to the Elysium of the crown (in the Marlovian vein), the Lancasters are impressed with the hardships and burdens of kingship. "O polished perturbation! Golden care" is Hal's address to the crown he finds beside his sleeping father. And after his father's denunciation, in his own defense he proceeds to recount what he actually had said. The golden crown is carnivorous: it eats the bearer up, as it has fed upon the body of his father:

> if it did infect my blood with joy
> Or swell my thoughts to any strain of pride,
> If any rebel or vain spirit of mine
> Did with the least affection of a welcome
> Give entertainment to the might of it.
> (170–74)

This oath, sworn with gravity and determination, pleases the father in two ways; it shows that his own labors have been appreciated, and that like himself Hal will be a serious ruler. Through their very sense of guilt and responsibility, added to determination, the Lancasters show a capacity for effective rule. The original sin, so dominant in the first tetralogy and looming in the second, has been purged through the very father-son ideal that is at the heart of Shakespeare's political ethic. The crown sat uneasily upon the head of the father. Bolingbroke, as the original man in the middle, had to assume the guilt of historical action. But that guilt has been broken. To his son the crown will descend with better quiet,

> Better opinion, better confirmation;
> For all the soil of the achievement goes
> With me into the earth.
>
> (189–91)

Henry is the scapegoat who carries the sins away. But his burden has been eased by his son's proving his right to succession. Henry IV does not die as a tragic figure, nor as a Christ-figure who simply absorbs the blow. At the end, as with Henry VIII, Henry IV's victory is historical. His action at a crucial moment of historical change, rather than being doomed by a sense of life that fears all doing, is justified in his son. As Henry VIII exclaims with pride and praises his Maker, So Henry IV finds his life's work vindicated, and cries out "Laud be to God." Where he does this is important. Waning fast, he asks in what room he fainted. Told it is called the Jerusalem room, he rejoices and then explains that he was once told he would die in Jerusalem, which he had thought to mean the Holy Land. Some critics have considered this to be a "juggling prophecy" which robs Henry IV of any contentment and shows him in the end to be a defeated man. Correct reading of this scene and Henry's attitude would seem to dispose of that interpretation. Far from being a juggling prophecy, it places the seal of approval on his actions. If he could not go to Jerusalem, Jerusalem came to him. And as in *Henry VIII*, there is some religious confirmation of this man who faced with resolution and courage the bitter choices that the new times presented to him.

This tetralogy is at the core of the larger developments of the study of time in the Renaissance. It shows, as in Spenser, the basic Elizabethan reinvestment in the ways of succession. In Dante, we recall, all rightness comes from God, and not through the lines of succession. We do not have to go back as far as Dante for that. Samuel Daniel, whom some have thought Shakespeare followed in his historical vision, also sees a controlling providence at work in the lines of English kings. After the superb attainment of Edward III and the promise of his sons, disaster strikes when the Black Prince predeceases his father and the throne is left to a child.

> But now the Scepter, in this glorious state,
> Supported with strong power and victories,
> Was left unto a Child, ordain'd by fate
> To stay the course of what might grow too hie:

> Here was a stop, that Greatness did abate,
> When powre upon so weake a base did lie.
> For, least good fortune should presume too farre,
> Such oppositions interposed are.

The world is still governed by the inscrutable powers that allow man his glory but are jealous when it seems to continue too long, and for the same reason as in Dante: then he will believe that he, and not these mastering powers, is the measure of things. But Shakespeare's vision differs even from that of Daniel. There is a kind of human effectiveness that does not act in opposition to the great powers of the world, but, as in the *Oresteia*, seems willing to give them their place of honor and their due of guilt, and the sweat of scrupulous preoccupation with law and government. This effectiveness is not of the Yorkist-Clytemnestra type, whose brag and insolence merely add to the process of retribution they thought they were breaking, but neither does it share the vision that utterly despairs of any redemption in time. That man can act safely in time—however harrowing and difficult it might be—is the credo of Shakespeare's development in the second tetralogy. Importantly, then, where argument of time is seriously used, it works to dissolve the hold of original sin.

Also related to the development of time in the Renaissance is the fact that a secular paideia replaces the Christian. In the Dante of the *Commedia*, man is a truer man the less he has of manliness, and the more he regains of the purity, innocence, and sense of life's coherence that a child has. As in other Renaissance works fundamentally concerned with education, so in Shakespeare's second tetralogy, the ideal formation takes place strictly between father and son. The older figure leads the son to maturity, responsibility, and order. Time is redeemed when this secular paideia functions, just as time is forfeited in the *Inferno* and in *Richard III* when that process is destroyed. In two speeches, one of which is memorable, Hal vows to maintain the processes of succession that his father feared were broken. Taking to himself the crown that (as he believed) killed his father, Hal affirms his right to it and his willingness to defend it:

> and put the world's whole strength
> Into one giant arm, it shall not force
> This lineal honour from me. This from thee
> Will I to mine leave, as 'tis left to me.
>
> (44–47)

We have already observed the "lineal honour" operating in the several reformations of the son, especially in *Part Two*, and also indirectly in the many echoes and resemblances passed on from father to son. Falstaff, especially, courts disappointment when he seeks to insert himself between the father-son relation.

The same order of stability that Hal comes to represent is absent from the worlds of Hotspur and Falstaff, but, significantly, they can be validly discussed in the temporal terms we have established. Hotspur is Hal's foil not only in reaped honors, but also in awareness. Hal's broad-gauged participation in many levels of existence is a kind of fortunate fall. While it seems to present him with greater difficulties ("most subject is the fattest soil to weeds") it also indicates greater possibilities—the "sparks of better hope"—which his father quite early detects. Separate and diffuse, his multiple identities can be damaging, but unified they show greater tolerance, broader perspectives, and a disposition to embrace life. Hotspur, or course, has none of these qualities. He is caught in that older way of reducing life to ultimate alternatives: honor or death, "or sink, or swim!" This tendency derives from his basic devaluation of life's normal activities and his fierce devotion to those moments of combat when all will be determined. Before battle he has no time for the letters brought by a messenger—"I cannot read them now":

> O gentlemen, the time of life is short!
> To spend that shortness basely were too long
> If life did ride upon a dial's point,
> Still ending at the arrival of an hour.
> An if we live, we live to tread on kings;
> If die, brave death, when princes die with us!
> (5.2.80–87)

His code of honor actually compels him to seek out dangerous situations:

> Send danger from the east unto the west,
> So honour cross it from the north to south,
> And let them grapple. O, the blood more stirs
> To rouse a lion than to start a hare!
> (1.3.195–98)

Hotspur is a man possessed, and when he speaks it is rarely to others, but rather out of some demonic trance within himself. These words, for instance, spoken at a council of war, are not really addressed to the group. Some inner jockey is spurring him on, and the crowd stands back in amazement at his frenzy. Northumberland, his father, provides the actor's cue:

> Imagination of some great exploit
> Drives him beyond the bounds of patience.
>
> (199–200)

But Percy proceeds:

> By heaven, methinks it were an easy leap
> To pluck bright honour from the pale-fac'd moon,
> Or dive into the bottom of the deep,
> Where fadom line could never touch the ground,
> And pluck up drowned honour by the locks,
> So he that doth redeem her thence might wear
> Without corrival all her dignities.

Worcester, his uncle, grows somewhat impatient at all of this fantasy:

> He apprehends a world of figures here,
> But not the form of what he should attend.
>
> (201–10)

With Hal, however, despite his own kind of isolation, we have none of this blind imagination. He seems to see better into people and situations: "I know you all . . ." And while he is deluded in thinking that he is in control of the situation (other forces must help effect his regeneration), still his presence in the easy world of jokes and stories, of small beer, provides a larger perspective from which to view the ludicrous warrior-myths and pride of the Glendowers and Hotspurs. In *1 Henry IV*, when Falstaff tells of the spreading rebellion, his very telling satirizes the spectacular pretensions of the soldier clan:

> That same mad fellow of the North, Percy, and he of Wales that gave Amamon the bastinado, and made Lucifer cuckold, and swore the devil his true liegeman upon the cross of a Welsh hook—what a plague call you him?
>
> (2.4.369–73)

Hal picks up the marvelous puncturing, completing Falstaff's similar description of Douglas, "that runs a-horseback up a hill perpendicular—"

> PRINCE: He that rides at high speed and with his pistol kills a sparrow flying.
> FALSTAFF: You have hit it.
> PRINCE: So did he never the sparrow.
>
> (378–82)

His sense of fun and humor is sparkling when he puts Francis' inarticulateness on parade or when he makes fun of Percy:

> That ever this fellow should have fewer words than a parrot,
> and yet the son of a woman! His industry is upstairs and down-
> stairs, his eloquence the parcel of a reckoning. I am not yet of
> Percy's mind, the Hotspur of the North; he that kills me some
> six or seven dozen of Scots at a breakfast, washes his hands, and
> says to his wife, "Fie upon this quiet life! I want work!" "O
> my sweet Harry," says she, "how many hast thou kill'd to-
> day?" "Give my roan horse a drench," says he, and answers
> "Some fourteen," an hour after, "a trifle, a trifle." I prithee call
> in Falstaff.
>
> (110–22)

The prince too knows that Hotspur apprehends a world of figures, and not what he should attend. His parody of Hotspur emphasizes his lack of responsiveness, his lack of consecutiveness. All consumed in his own world, time is unimportant. Rather than answering his wife's question (still in Hal's parody) he gives an order instead, and one hour later registers his response. There is strong evidence in the play that Hal's comic version of Hotspur is not inaccurate.

With the exception of the material in the section [in *The Renaissance Discovery of Time*] on "The Dramatic Exploitation of Time," I have generally ignored the interesting problems of the sequences of actual plot time. But because of the conceptual value of the presentation of dramatic time in *1 Henry IV*, I make an exception here, Mable Buland has studied the problems and development of double time in Elizabethan drama, with particular attention to Shakespeare. In brief, she states that double time in the plays results from "an attempt to give the effect of close continuity of action, and to use at the same time a plot requiring the lapse of months or years." I find that the use of double time in *Henry IV* serves the added purpose of reflecting the two young heroes' varying attitudes toward life. Miss Buland summarizes the plot-times of the play:

> In *1* and *2 Henry IV* . . . Shakespeare reverted to the epic type
> of the chronicle, but not to the kind of construction used in the
> *Henry VI* plays; for into the episodic scenes of Hotspur's rebel-
> lion he has woven a comic story possessing such close continuity
> that a semblance of coherence is imparted to the whole play. In
> *1 Henry IV*, we hear Falstaff and Prince Harry plan to take a

purse "to-morrow night in Eastcheap" (1.2); we see the early morning robbery, we enjoy the supper scene after the night's adventures; we hear the Prince resolve, "I'll to the court in the morning" (2.4.595); and presently we find the son and father together (3.2). It is then arranged that "on Wednesday next" the prince shall set forward with his troops, and a few days later, at the battle of Shrewsbury, the play is concluded. Nevertheless, the affairs of Hotspur, which should be concurrent with those of the Prince of Wales, cover a period of three months, and their long-time extension is clearly indicated.

Although Hotspur's activities cover a longer period of time, they do not suggest continuity. They represent a disrupted sequence of heightened moments: they are crisis episodes. Human interest is kept up by the sheer eccentricity and "humor" of the wild-eyed devotee of soldier's honor. Yet there is no suggestion of the fuller life, or any interest other than honor (which has a strong echo of cracking heads). Time between the crucial episodes is of little value:

> Uncle, adieu. O, let the hours be short
> Till fields and blows and groans applaud our sport!
>
> (1.2.301–2)

The prince, on the other hand, is involved in the more quotidian world of community and consecutive experience. His plot time, if briefer, is more continuous, and therefore more open to extension. Hotspur's time, while covering a longer period, is actually contracted into short moments: it is more suggestive of the tragic world of passion to which his end is the consummation.

Beneath Hotspur's devotion to crisis-time is a certain devaluation of the small things in extended time. Underlying his stance is a desperate skepticism that comes out in his last speech:

> But thoughts the slaves of life, and life time's fool,
> And time, that takes survey of all the world,
> Must have a stop.
>
> (5.4.81–83)

As his approach to time has indicated and as this final turning away shows, Hotspur's attitudes do not promote the kind of temporal stability and controlling powers that Shakespeare valued in his more life-seeking monarchs.

In the histories, Falstaff is Shakespeare's prime creation of a negligent greatness. Hal is determined to redeem the time and move against the tempest of commotion that drops on his "unarmed head." But there is strong evidence that Falstaff misdeems the time and is by his own admission heinously unprovided. He is the latter spring, and the all-hallown summer. His desire outlives performance. The man of incongruities and incomprehensible lies, whose predilection was for the latter end of a fray and the beginning of a feast, brought laughter in *Part One*. His sheer extravagances were rewarded, and his inconsecutiveness was much to the point. But a move persists to expose Falstaff, whether after Gadshill, or when Poins and Hal oversee him in *Part Two*. And like the Wife of Bath, Falstaff is an aging, melancholy comic hero, beset by occasional religious anxiety, but also driven by hard economic motivation. Underneath his inconsequence there is a hard line of practical shrewdness: " 'When thou art King' runs like a refrain through what he has to say, and reveals the anxieties beneath the jesting . . . What is to happen when the old King dies? That, as we are reminded time and time again in this scene, is the leading problem of Falstaff's existence" (J. Dover Wilson, *The Fortunes of Falstaff*). The hope is that the prince will spare him the reckoning of his more extravagant ways, that the prince will provide and set Falstaff's accounts in order.

The call to account is crucial to the argument of time. It is the fatal moment for which one must prepare, the sick hour that Richard's surfeit brought, the bitter realization against which Shakespeare warns the young man in the sonnets, and the crucial hour of combat for which the interview with his father prepares Hal. The call to account is the inevitable summons that breaks through illusion and presents a hard world of reality. But Falstaff, we are told at once in *1 Henry IV*, is superfluous in demanding the time of day. "What a devil has thou to do with the time of day," unless the signs and acts of pleasure were fitting marks for the world of time. Attached to the prince, Falstaff is the allowed jester: he never is called to pay. The prince may have called the hostess to a reckoning many a time, but he never called Falstaff to pay his part. "No, I'll give thee thy due, thou has paid all there" (1.2.59). The prince's credit redeems Falstaff's activities. As Gadshill, the spotter explains: his team of robbers includes some who are involved in the robbery for sport's sake, "that would (if matters should be look'd into) for their own credit sake make all whole" (2.1.79). Falstaff's world is a merry play world. Watch tonight, pray tomorrow . . . "A play extempore" is the proper happening for those who live by their wits. After the robbery, when the play world has been interrupted by the knocking of the sheriff's men, Hal engages his word that Falstaff (hidden fast asleep behind the arras) will answer the complaints.

The prince promises that the money will be paid back "with advantage," and persists in being the good "angel" to Falstaff.

Falstaff is ill-prepared for the emulative struggle to which the prince is called. The either/or challenge of Hotspur which Hal must answer is for Falstaff merely

> Rare words! brave world! Hostess, my breakfast, come.
> O, I could wish this tavern were my drum!
>
> (3.3.228–29)

He is somewhat reluctant to settle accounts, especially in a world of struggle and real threats; in London's taverns his wit and verbal skills could get him by, but not in combat: "Though I could scape shot-free at London, I fear the shot here. Here's no scoring but upon the pate" (5.3.30–32). As the moment of battle approaches, Falstaff asks Hal's assistance. But Hal is not colossal enough to bestride him in battle: "Say thy prayers, and farewell."

> FALSTAFF: I would 'twere bedtime, Hal, and all well.
> PRINCE: Why, thou owest God a death.
> FALSTAFF: 'Tis not due yet, I would be loath to pay him before
> his day. Why need I be so forward with him that calls
> not on me?
>
> (5.1.126–30)

While it would be foolhardy to rush toward that reckoning, still the postponement he seeks here is only part of the larger practice of deferral that is typical of Falstaff throughout both parts of *Henry IV*.

In the battle Hal significantly does not bestride Falstaff, but rather his father. And when Falstaff pulls the bottle of sack from where his pistol should be, the prince rebukes his poor timing: "What, is it a time to jest and dally now?" (5.3.57). The preparation for rejection proceeds—even if premature and bound to be deferred. When Hal sees the fallen Falstaff, whom he mistakenly believes to be dead, the prince hardly expresses any regret:

> O, I should have a heavy miss of thee
> If I were much in love with vanity!
>
> (5.4.105–6)

Again the Lancastrian seriousness returns to judge the frivolity of those whom they reject or oppose. But Falstaff is not dead, only counterfeiting, and he springs to life to pull off his most incredible stunt: claiming he killed Hotspur. The claim has all the more chance of success in the world of *Part*

One, the more preposterous and patently incredible it is. Falstaff lands on his feet, and the prince again uses his credit to spare him a reckoning:

> For my part, if a lie may do thee grace,
> I'll gild it with the happiest terms I have.
>
> (161–62)

In *Part Two*, the law is not so easily fobbed off. The Lord Chief Justice holds the keys to this terrain, as the law-bound Cato did in the *Purgatorio*. He is just as severe in his retention of the past, and the object of his implacability is Falstaff: "It is not a confident brow, nor the throng of words that come with such more than impudent sauciness from you, can thrust me from a level consideration" (2.1.121–24). He is determined that Falstaff pay his debt to Hostess Quickly "both in purse and person." Earlier the Chief Justice showed that he at least had not forgotten the events of Gadshill: "Your days's service at Shrewsbury hath a little gilded over your night's exploit on Gadshill. You may thank th' unquiet time for your quiet o'erposting that action" (1.2.168–71). Falstaff's pretensions of youthfulness, and his brawling are unseemly to the serious man of order, "Doth this become you place, your time and business?" (2.1.73). Such a complaint will be echoed by the newly crowned Henry V: "How ill white hairs become a fool and jester!" (5.5.52).

Falstaff is ill attended in *Part Two*. Like the Chief Justice, the prince's brother John is not an ideal audience for his antics. He warns Falstaff of the danger he is running by his eccentric ways:

> Now, Falstaff, where have you been all the while?
> When everything is ended, then you come.
> These tardy tricks of yours will, on my life,
> One time or other break some gallows' back.
>
> (4.3.29–32)

For one scene only, prior to rejection time, Falstaff and Hal appear together in *Part Two* (2.4). And as in *Part One*, Poins and the prince have designed a trap to expose Falstaff. The directions of both plays seem toward Falstaff's exposure. But in *Part Two*, much of the former gaiety has passed out of the scene, and it ends unsatisfactorily and unresolved. The final impression is one of time profaned. Indeed, it is "Falstaff, good night."

Although Falstaff has not altogether lost his charm in *Part Two*, he is no longer so outlandishly inconsequential. He has acquired authority, and he uses his new employment to deliver himself from the officers of the Chief Justice. But as he becomes more consequential in speech and behavior, he becomes more of a real problem and hence more open to rejection: "You speak as having power to do wrong" (2.1.141).

Debts past due, of which the Chief Justice is the unrelenting collector, are closing in on Falstaff. There are signs that his good angel of the past will no longer pay the reckoning. One indication of Hal's future behavior is in his father's accusation that under his reign any kind of hoodlum and criminal would find refuge: "England shall double gild his treble guilt." The same term of covering was used by Hal in *Part One*, and by the Chief Justice in *Part Two* to describe the royal credit that was redeeming Falstaff's carelessness and illegality. The father's charge is pointed. But rather than to Falstaff, it is to the Chief Justice that Hal gives his hand, "you shall be as father to my youth." In *Parts One* and *Two* Falstaff loses out to time and the Law. As in Dante's *Purgatorio*, these two principles, part of the argument of time, necessitate a rejection that continues to be debated.

It is quite natural that we should recoil at Falstaff's rejection, just as we did at Virgil's—even though the latter seemed to represent more positive ideals. After Romanticism, as Professor Langbaum has shown, the quandary of moral categories and sympathetic character seems only to have become thicker. Naive readers have continued to protest, and overly severe teachers have continued to pursue rigorously the textual logic that requires dismissal. However much we might wish to see Falstaff's presumption deflated and delight in the dramatic effects that build up to his final exposure, however much we might be aware that Falstaff's egotism personally intrudes on the proper and serious business of governing a country, and however much we are brought to realize that lurking on the verge of Falstaff's domain is disorder, crime, and even murder, still it is not without regret that we see the world deprived of his good force. It is this to which Edmund Wilson responds when he joins in association Falstaff and the later tragic figures, Lear and Antony. In their loss a great force has gone out of the world.

Falstaff's merits become apparent, not in contrast with the virtues required of the monarch, but when set next to the lesser characters who seem to thrive. Shallow, a simple fool except where money is concerned, is everything that Falstaff is not. Ever in the rearward of the fashion, this country squire still has more than Bardolph for security. His beefs and Falstaff's lack of provisions presents another of those occasions that inform against one, those bitter lessons that reveal a clear reality. Shallow sounds the depths of his name. He is nostalgic and backward-looking to a past he never had. In his great soliloquy (3.4), Falstaff has nothing but scorn (and some designs) for this lying old man, who in his youth was no way like himself. He only sang outmoded songs and never had the courage, enterprise, or wit to be the blade he later imagined himself to be. He was a hanger-on, one who circled around the outskirts of the tumult. He was never at the center of things; he never took the risks of the thrust. Yet, now he is wealthy and Falstaff desperately in need of provisions. This speech shows Falstaff's virtues in proper dialectic; Shallow's triumphant narrowness is degraded in contrast with the risk-taking Falstaff. It was Falstaff who ventured, who drew laughs, who was wit itself and the cause of wit in other men.

Falstaff had always misdeemed the time and ignored the need to provide prudently. And while there was always a latent cynicism in his profane detraction from heroics, still it is only in his advanced age, when he sees fools provided for, that he grimly sets about to hunt for himself: "If the young dace be a bait for the old pike, I see no reason in the law of the nature but I may snap at him [Shallow]. Let time shape, and there an end" (3.2.356–59). Falstaff can hardly inspire his wonted affection in us when he speaks of the "law of nature." This latter-day lapse into an opportunistic ethic, similar to that of the Yorkists, is a startling reversal from the earlier gaiety (for all its undertone of future gain). His freedom has become victimized by its own excess and desperately converts from happy inconsequence into hard calculation; perennially out of season, Falstaff too late in life adopts a grim code of provision. And ironically, it is this final resolve to take advantage of the time, that element which he had so grandiosely scanted, which helps to make Falstaff dramatically ripe for rejecting.

THE SIGNIFICANCE OF TIME IN SHAKESPEARE'S HISTORIES

True to its form, Shakespeare's argument of time exhorts response. And the response, as proclaimed in the sonnets, involves a faith in the augmentative potential of the ways of succession. Wherever these ways are open, and man places his confidence in them, children and fame are valuable counters in the war against nothingness and oblivion. And this perhaps is one of the values of the argument of time: it provides a bridge between the private voice of the sonnets and the more public world of the drama. It concentrates on the problems that help to make the histories intense personal, as well as political drama. But it also gives larger scope to the virtues of good government: prudence and responsibility and even decorum are more than that when they are stabilizing guards against a chaotic and destructive world of willful vanity, negligence, and nothingness. The argument of time provides such enlargements for Shakespeare's political ethic.

We have already had occasion to observe this double dimension of time in the Renaissance: it is a cosmic discovery that translates itself into schedule; with fervor it combines practicality. These aspects of time in the Renaissance help to explain the division on modern criticism over Shakespeare's successful House of Lancaster. Whether defending Richard II or Falstaff, men like Yeats or Bradley are repulsed by the calculation, priggishness, and prudence of the Lancasters. "To suppose that Shakespeare preferred men who deposed his king is to suppose that Shakespeare judged men with the eyes of a Municipal Councillor weighing the merits of a Town Clerk; and that had he been by when Verlaine cried out from his bed, "Sir, you have been made by the stroke of a pen but I have been made by the breath of God," he would have though the Hospital Superintendent the better man" ("At Stratford-on-Avon" in *Essays and Introductions*). Indeed, there is part of us that wishes Yeats to be right, that feels uncomfortable whenever we insist too pompously on the correctness of deposition or dismissal. But, at the same time, we also feel that Yeats, bristling under the divisions of his own time, has stripped the growth and significance of Hal of half the interest it holds for us. He belittles the prudence, but he forgets the cosmic issues of time and nothingness against which prudence is a defense. He mocks the decisions of the public man, but he forgets the private setting for those decisions. In short, Yeats is prevented from seeing the crucial nature of time in the Renaissance. Time is a principle of reality that limits human freedom, but it also heightens reality. It is these deeper issues in Hal's development that the argument of time brings out. Yet Yeats is historically percipient. Just that severe division which would eventually come about between Verlaine's spirited vanity and the dull Municipal Councillor has its roots in the Renaissance triumph of time. And Shakespeare's own tragedies will show the split that Yeats detected in the histories. But for a while, with Shakespeare, as with other Renaissance writers, when time was still an important and fervent discovery, the union of energy and control was still possible. Rabelais could have his education of Gargantua and the freer air of the Abbey. The practical results of the discovery of time could still be exciting, especially when man was trying to liberate himself from an unworthy torpor, or in Shakespeare's case, from older ways that no longer served the modern prince. The modern world, especially in literature, would like to return to the world before time became a pressure and a commodity. Yet it was just this discovery of time that is intrinsic to the nature and accomplishments of the Renaissance.

The first tetralogy shows the transition from the high point of England's medieval achievement to the first Renaissance English monarch. So, too, the second tetralogy deals with the "change of times," as it moves from a king whose values are medieval to one whose values are more like those of the Tudors (whether represented by Henry VII or the Cranmer oration in *Henry VIII*). In the first tetralogy Henry V is the last of the medieval kings; in the second, he is the glorious representative, shown in his growth and development, of the modern notions of realism, effectiveness, comprehensiveness of appeal. His contrast with Hotspur transcends mere competition between coevals; it is rather between two different ways of life. There is more in Hal that seeks and deserves survival; there is more in Hal that is in tune with the nature of the world and the demands of the time. With all of his tremendous vitality and spirited vision, Percy is still food for worms.

> Ill-weav'd ambition, how much art thou shrunk!
> When that this body did contain a spirit,
> A kingdom for it was too small a bound;
> But now two paces of the vilest earth
> Is room enough.
> (*1 Henry IV* 5.4.88–92)

Hal's vision includes human limitations and vulnerabilities. His spirit is not as doom-eager and death-insistent as the tragically motivated chivalric and aristocratic Hotspur. J. Dover Wilson's comments on these lines, especially "ill-weaved ambition," are suggestive: "Such is the quality of Hotspur's ambition . . . and such the language of Shakespeare, the wool-dealer's son, who well knew that cloth loosely woven was especially apt to shrink." Shakespeare, the wool-dealer's son, finds the values and personality of a Hotspur inappropriate for true management, stability, and safety in the world. There is not enough in Hotspur that seeks life over death. He shows too much willfulness, too great a reluctance to adjust one's spirit to the realities of existence. And one of the great realities is time.

Continuing to follow larger historical suggestions, it has been clear from our study that the sense of time as an urgent pressure was coincidental with the rise of bourgeois society and the middle class. More to the point, time figures prominently in the formation of middle-class values. It suggests an external world of real limitations, against which one must make provisions if he is to be spared an unsatisfactory reckoning. If, then, Shakespeare's England witnessed the great alliance under the Tudors between the throne and the middle class, it is clear why time is so important a force in Shakespeare's second tetralogy. Historical in value, the history plays reflect historical reality: Hal is the embodiment of the Tudor revolution in values that Shakespeare sought to dramatize. Against the bedeviled turmoil of a

Hotspur, he sets Falstaffian life. But against Falstaff's nihilism, he sets a modified code of honor and historical continuity that is a consolidation of the traditions of the old in harmony with present realities. In his most stirring affirmation in *2 Henry IV*, Hal draws a particularly English bridge over the gap of historical change, uniting in a single unit the old and the new. "The tide of blood in me," he confesses,

> Hath proudly flow'd in vanity till now.
> Now doth it turn and ebb back to the sea,
> Where it shall mingle with the state of
>   floods
> And flow henceforth in formal majesty.
>
> (5.2.129–33)

Despite the disruption of Bolingbroke's revolution, despite the new realism of his house, continuity has been maintained—and more than maintained, gloriously advanced. Aristocratic and bourgeois, Hal represents the great tendency toward amalgamation of virtues that we had already observed in Spenser, and had further seen to be crucial to the problem of time in the Renaissance.

For Harry Levin, in his important essay "English Literature of the Renaissance," Bacon's "Merchants of Light" symbolize "the belated yet determining role that Englishmen played in the Renaissance, the mediating practicality that reshaped its ideas into those of the Enlightenment." While we could see in "Merchants of Light" the several facets of time, it is the phrase "mediating practicality" that is justified by many points in this study, and which the history plays dramatize. We could say that the fundamental contrast between the House of York and the House of Lancaster was the absence of this mediating practicality in the former. They too unreservedly in Shakespeare's plays took over the Machiavellian line without submitting to the larger needs of time and place. In the Marlovian vein, they were too unmitigated in their adoptions, without transforming their desires to the larger needs of life and order. If Richard II, Henry VI, and Falstaff were too negligent or improvident, the Richards of the first tetralogy were too aggressive and belligerent. And yet Shakespeare, and the directions of English thought in the Renaissance, sensed the importance of time and the need for man to manage it effectively, to husband it. Somewhere between the premature reliance on being and the unscrupulous seizure of time must, unfortunately, lie the difficult shadow area of proper action. Man can act safely in time, but it involves heavy responsibilities and burdens, with the quieter rewards and consolations of the ways of peace and succession.

Indeed, given the Baconian context of Professor Levin's remarks, the second tetralogy—with its faith in a virtuous control of experience stabilized by the successful father-son relationship, with its recognition of a hard objective reality and the need for man to be modest in the face of his vulnerable exposure, yet through this submission to the laws of nature to be able, in turn, to control experience—the later group of history plays seems to have found its proper setting.

The Dialectic of Right and Power in *Henry IV, Part 1*

Michael McCanles

Once become king, Bolingbroke legitimizes his tenuous claim to the throne through the rites and appearances of order and respectability. In doing so, he confronts in the rebellious Northumberland, Harry Percy, and Worcester his own mirror image come back to haunt him. Both Henry and the rebels convert their base motives upwards, thereby inviting a reconversion downward. The Percy faction juggles with such motives when Hotspur insists that their rebellion will restore the honor they lost in helping Henry depose Richard. He calls it a "shame" "that men of your nobility and power" should have cooperated with "this canker Bolingbroke" in putting "down Richard, that sweet lovely rose." "Yet," he continues, "time serves wherein you may redeem / Your banish'd honours, and restore yourselves / Into the good thoughts of the world again" (1.3.165ff.). This kind of reasoning appeals to Hotspur, who conceives actions and results almost entirely as a function of reputation and honor. In the same scene, however, Worcester more accurately describes their motives. He knows that "the King will always think him in our debt, / And think we think ourselves unsatisfy'd, / Till he hath found a time to pay us home" (280–82). That Worcester predicts (correctly) how the king will himself predict (also correctly) their justifications for rebellion, shows that they are both of a kind, for they think exactly alike. Henry's displays of political respectability, as well as his former allies' rebellion under the banner of restoring usurped monarchal rights, are thus versions of each other.

From *Dialectical Criticism and Renaissance Literature.* © 1975 by the Regents of the University of California. The University of California Press, 1975.

Both king and rebels judge themselves and others within mutually exclusive categories of simple right and wrong, high and low motives, respectable and unrespectable actions. For Hotspur, the respectable equals insistence on nice points of honor, downright commitment to blows and battle, and exaggerated disdain of feminine company. The unrespectable for him is anything that savors of devious policy (the king), or frivolity (the prince). In the king himself, we find an almost bourgeois anxiety for family name and honor besmirched in the gutter. In judging by such simplistic ethical categories, both are unprepared for the ironies of debunking to which they are vulnerable, because these categories conceal their secret sharing in base motives with those whom they execrate and oppose. Thus, Henry's attempts to set himself on the side of order and respectability, and Hotspur and Hal on the side of disorder and tainted action merely invite back upon himself further rebellion. On Hotspur's part, rebellion's pretensions to "honor" mirror Henry's own and also debunk them. Prince Hal's rebellion inoculates moral respectability against the moral decay that it masks in both king and rebels, and becomes therefore both the disease and the cure. Hal's truancy is truly what his father calls it, "a secret doom out of my blood" through which God will "breed revengement and a scourge for me" (3.2.6–7). Hal is of course the appropriate son for Henry, mirroring back to him his own defaults, unmasking his father's "respectability."

In Falstaff, we behold a parody of order and respectability "gross as a mountain, open, palpable" (2.4.221). Falstaff does not present us simply with the embodiment of debauchery and feeding set off against the king's respectability. There is another aspect of Falstaff, not nearly enough commented on, that tempts me to see him as cut quite univocally out of the same cloth. This aspect is Falstaff's hunger for respectability. No one quotes scripture in Shakespeare more than Falstaff, and no one is more a master of the odds and ends of manners and morals, of sermons and proverbs, and of pious exhortation. Falstaff's moral piquancy lies, therefore, not simply in his representing holiday as opposed to Henry's sobriety. On the contrary, his mastery, no less than Henry's, of the rhetoric of moral exhortation and the stances of self-righteous complacency make him an embodiment of moral ambiguity that is formidable to deal with. When Falstaff parodies King Henry's sermon to his son (to come in 3.2), we perceive that he parodies himself as well. And yet Falstaff distinguishes himself from Henry in his sometimes complacent, sometimes anguished recognition of the gulf between his high pretenses and the seedy reality. This is the gulf that Henry is committed to denying, that his self-righteousness indeed exists to deny.

Falstaff's mask of moral probity is only one of the masks he puts on and takes off with serene ease and celerity. But if his ability to create for himself various roles and the appropriate rhetoric debunks the actors in the main plot, then Hal debunks the debunker by continually unmasking various personae. When Falstaff says to Hal, "Do not thou when thou art king hang a thief," and Hal answers, "No, thou shalt," Falstaff is immensely taken with the role of the hanging judge. When Hal corrects him, and says that Falstaff shall be himself a hangman, Falstaff has little trouble adjusting to this role too (1.2.59ff.). Hal's and Falstaff's understandings of this exchange are carefully distinguished. Hal can relish the moral ironies bound up in the idea of a thief hanging another thief in the name of justice, while Falstaff misses them completely. Hal's facility in wheeling to Falstaff's blind side to score marks him as the one character flexible enough to escape through the moral ambiguities thrust on all else by their attempts to deny such ambiguities. For Falstaff, as for the king, respectability can only be achieved by "hanging" the thief in himself through hanging other thieves.

When, still later in this scene, Falstaff sighs over the corruptions Hal has led him into, so much so that now he is "little better than one of the wicked," the prince immediately counters with "Where shall we take a purse tomorrow, Jack?" Falstaff easily reversed his field and answers " 'Zounds, where thou wilt, lad, I'll make one." Hal, the supreme connoisseur of Falstaff's moral juggling, comments "I see a good amendment of life in thee, from praying to purse-taking" (1.2.88ff.). Falstaff's rhetoric is complex here, for we cannot tell whether he only pretends to the hypocrisy that Hal has corrupted him, or whether he really believes it. Falstaff may at once savor the language of repentance and mock it. These two attitudes, far from being incompatible, are dialectically correlative. For Falstaff, like King Henry and Hotspur, is the first to condemn others whenever he can manufacture some sort of moral edge over them. When anyone in this play affects one side of a moral antinomy in conscious contradistinction to its opposite, he is doomed to enact both opposites, and not know it. Falstaff alternately mocks sober age from the viewpoint of youthful exuberance, and also assumes the persona of that sobriety, castigating youthful debauchery and corruption. Falstaff's counterpart, Hotspur, manages much of the time to convey a deliberately important air of conscious responsibility and no-nonsense dedication to purposeful action, a kind of adolescent pomposity that scoffs at play and women. As such, he is merely the Falstaffian roughneck affecting his antimask. And so there is really a true, and not simply an ironic sense, in which Falstaff is youth and Hotspur age.

Shakespeare presents Hotspur's rebelliousness as a twitchy subjection to certain drives, actions, and reactions, something like a tic. For instance, all of his enemies evolve into the affected popinjay whom Hotspur mimics when Shakespeare first introduces him. He is adept at delineating the affected courtier with all the malevolent relish of Tom Sawyer anatomizing a Sunday-school goody-goody: "He was perfumed like a milliner, / And 'twixt his finger and his thumb he held / A pouncet-box, which ever and anon / he gave his nose, and took't away again / . . . and still he smil'd and talk'd . . ." (1.3.35–40). When he is waxing enflamed against the king he categorizes him in the same way: "Why, what a candy deal of courtesy / This fawning greyhound then did proffer me!"(1.3.247–48). Still later, when reading a letter counseling caution from one of his erstwhile allies, he bursts out with: " 'Zounds, and I were now by this rascal I could brain him with his lady's fan"(2.3.22–23). The ironic parallels between Hotspur and Falstaff on the subject of honorable action go well beyond the two as representatives of excess and deficiency respectively. Though Hotspur and Falstaff are both facile in creating roles for themselves, the essential difference lies between one who is flexible in his role-playing and one who is not. The rigidity of Hotspur's stance allows him to make anarchy in the name of honor and be incapable of distinguishing the two. Unlike Falstaff, he cannot doff his masks when they no longer serve, and his enslavement to these stances he shares with the king.

Falstaff undercuts both of them, in refusing to be bound by any stance, either moral or self-consciously antimoral, and is flexible enough to shift according to the demands of the situation. In this respect, he acts as a kind of lightning rod for Hal, absorbing the malign possibilities of moral equivocation within himself so as to free Hal from these. Therefore, when Hal takes the stool and begins to play his father (2.4.428), he equivocates just as Falstaff does, but with a difference, His mimicking both his father and his boon companion demonstrates his independence of the values of both. When Hal, his own voice speaking through the persona of his father, banishes plump Jack Falstaff, he of necessity banishes his father also, because both old men share the moral ambiguity which their moral self-righteousness attempts to hide and only succeeds in revealing.

"To Demand the Time of Day": Prince Hal

Elliot Krieger

From his first moment on stage Hal disputes Falstaff's need, even his right, to know the time:

> FALSTAFF: Now, Hal, what time of day is it, lad?
> HAL: What a devil hast thou to do with the time of day? unless
> hours were cups of sack, and minutes capons, and clocks
> the tongues of bawds, and dials the signs of leaping-
> houses, and the blessed sun himself a fair hot wench in
> flame-color'd taffata; I see no reason why thou shouldst
> be so superfluous to demand the time of day.
>
> (1.2.1–12)

Hal responds more vehemently than the contents of Falstaff's request demand, indicating, as Roy Battenhouse has pointed out, that Falstaff has raised both a question and an issue. Falstaff's question about the time of day seems to encroach upon Hal's territory; Hal frightens Falstaff off as he might a poacher or a trespasser—the prince needs to maintain a boundary and a difference between himself and Falstaff. Hal here asserts and imposes the boundary between knowing and not knowing (perhaps between caring and not caring about) the time of day, but the terms through which Hal suggests Falstaff's indifference to time give the boundary between Hal and Falstaff a set of secondary meanings. By suggesting that Falstaff's interest in time—in anything—must be material, Hal accuses Falstaff of an inability

From *A Marxist Study of Shakespeare's Comedies*. © 1979 by Elliot Krieger. Macmillan Press Ltd., 1979.

to think in abstractions. He creates an image of a Falstaff obsessed with lust, gluttony, and debauchery, and, in doing so, Hal defends himself. Hal protects himself by proposing that, for Falstaff, concern with the time of day becomes obliterated in the continuous present of gluttonous satisfaction; Hal's own historical identity as part of a family of Machiavels, without legitimate title to the crown, is projected onto another's identity, is transformed from political into corporeal gluttony. By creating and then projecting the association of not knowing the time with debauchery and immediate consumption, Hal can maintain for himself the assurance that so long as he does know the time he will be free from Falstaffian contagion, he will be able to delay gratification and thereby control his environment and his destiny, his place in history. Hal never answers Falstaff's question.

Nor does Falstaff demand an answer. Instead of pursuing his initial question, Falstaff adopts the prince's verbal strategy of self-defense through polar opposition. He accepts indifference to the time of day and asserts dedication to the night, calling himself a man "of good government, being govern'd, as the sea is, by our noble and chaste mistress the moon" (27–9). This retort has left Hal vulnerable; should the prince still wish to maintain his opposition to Falstaff, he would have to develop a defense of the day's beauty, which for some reason he does not do—perhaps because defending the beauty of the sun would come too close, metaphorically, to a defense of the king's government, an argument he will not risk losing. Instead, Hal shifts ground and pronouns entirely, as he includes himself in Falstaff's image cluster of thievery, government, sun and moon:

> Thou sayest well, and it holds well too, for the fortune of *us*
> that are the moon's men doth ebb and flow like the sea, being
> govern'd, as the sea is, by the moon.
>
> (1.2.30–33)

With this shift from Falstaffian opponent to Falstaffian associate the prince shows us for the first time in the play his much-noted ambiguity, or, in the perhaps more appropriate term, ambivalence (the one term describes Shakespeare's motivation; the other, Hal's). Hal dissociates himself from, because he feels repulsed by, the materiality and sensuality of Falstaff's sense of time, which measures by appetite and desire, but Hal does not carry this attitude to its logical conclusion, he does not claim to represent and uphold the abstract of time of history. Hal's ambivalence allows him to join with Falstaff in attacking authority—"the day's beauty"—while never binding himself to appetite, "the night's body."

Through the two sides of his attitude toward indulgence, Hal enacts within the tavern so as to indulge his carnal and corporeal appetites—for food, drink, and perhaps sex, depending on what one means by calling the hostess of the tavern "to a reckoning many a time and oft" (49–50)—awhile he describes his life at the tavern as not a holiday interlude but a period of work and austerity reluctantly undertaken so as to consolidate and fortify his social stature within the primary world of history. Prince Hal, like other aristocratic protagonists, uses the second world as part of his strategy for maintaining authority in the primary world, but he does not accept the tavern as a retreat, a holiday interlude. He consciously opposes the intimations of timelessness and of charity with his own sense of hierarchy and propriety and with his cognizance of time. Hal, more conscious of the political function of retreat than the aristocratic protagonists in the double-world comedies, uses the tavern as a functioning term within the world of history. Hal maintains his own authority in the midst of indulgence rather than perpetrate the fiction that indulgence temporarily releases a whole society from the need for authority.

But the aristocratic authority that Hal maintains in the tavern does not entirely oppose him to all those without aristocratic stature. Hal's maintained authority does have *some* advantages for Falstaff, at lease in so far as Hal has "credit" enough to have "paid all" Falstaff's "part" (51–58). The aristocratic credit Hal gains through his authority relieves him of obligation to Falstaff and obliges him to acknowledge implicitly his historical, his future, responsibilities as the prince. Hal can both answer and not answer Falstaff's question about the time—he can reproach Falstaff for not needing to know without suggesting that he himself knows the time—but, because Falstaff knows the difference in stature between himself and the prince, as well as the advantages and dangers which that difference contains for him, he can both ask and not ask his question. Falstaff's question, therefore, contains an element of reproach, as if he means to taunt Hal for not knowing the time, to remind Hal that he has become dangerously close to an existence within the continuous present of appetite: "Indeed you come near me now, Hal" (13).

Falstaff repeats this reproach, adopting Hal's turn of phrase, later in the play when the two meet near Coventry on their way to battle. "What a devil dost thou in Warwickshire?", Falstaff asks the prince; then, turning to the Lord of Westmoreland, who accompanies the prince to the battlefield, Falstaff adds: "I thought your honor had already been at Shrewsbury" (4.2.50–53). Here, of course, Falstaff subtly but significantly reverses the terms and positions employed in his initial exchange with Hal. Falstaff now directly suggests that Hal has no concern with the time; he intimates that

Hal has again "come near" him by delaying his approach to the battle, by lagging behind in the safety of Coventry while Percy "is already in the field" (75). Although Falstaff's intimations about Hal's sense of historical responsibility have become quite direct—they approach accusation—Hal, in contrast with his vehement response during their first discussion about the time, responds to Falstaff with measured restraint and good-natured wit. In fact, Westmoreland parries Falstaff's thrust:

> Faith, Sir John, 'tis more than time that I were there [i.e. at Shrewsbury], and you too, but my powers are there already.
>
> (4.2.54–56)

Although the prince, too, encourages Falstaff to "make haste" (74), I think that Hal's consciousness has been divided. He has, by this point in the play, overcome his *dramatic* ambivalence toward the world of appetite, the tavern, but he cannot yet declare his resolution, perhaps because of the *moral* ambivalence, his combined sense of compassion and contempt for Falstaff's soldiers, that he maintains. Consequently, the official and historical side of Hal's consciousness, that part of Hal that uses the tavern for work rather than for indulgence, gets, in this scene, displaced onto the otherwise entirely superfluous Lord of Westmoreland. This displacement prevents Falstaff from knowing how conscious Hal has become of historical time and of his place in history; Falstaff, and to some extent the audience, therefore perceives the two sides of Hal's attitude toward history, toward the battle, as the attitudes of two different people. Both Shakespeare and Hal use the Lord of Westmoreland: Shakespeare uses him to prevent Falstaff from too early experiencing his separation from the prince; Hal uses him as an official spokesman, one who will enunciate the official and public policies that Hal has agreed upon to support but behind whom Hal can continue, when appropriate or advantageous, to jest and dally.

Hal's delegation to the Lord of Westmoreland of a portion of his public voice signifies both the authority that Hal maintains regarding other public figures in the drama (Hal and his father are the only characters who can successfully partition their own consciousnesses) and the bifold problem that confronts the prince each time history, through the regulations of the court, intervenes in the tavern. I call Hal's problem bifold because it has two separate and separable aspects: Hal must both commit himself to eventual participation in the world of historical time and he must determine when and how others, in court and tavern, will become aware that he understands his own responsibilities and that he has the capacity for action.

These two issues converge immediately after Hal's play-acting scene with Falstaff, as the sheriff, representing the authority inherent in the king-dom, enters the tavern. Hal has just, in his famous response to Falstaff's impassioned self-defense, declared both his present and eventual separation from Falstaff's sensual indulgences; I believe, however, that Hal says "I do, I will" (2.4.481) as a burst of dramatic bravura: I doubt the prince should really consciously control his destiny here, for he continues in the high spirits of good fellowship until the entry of the law. (Perhaps Falstaff somehow realizes the implications of Hal's outburst, and thus takes refuge from destiny in the primal narcissism of drunken sleep.) But Hal changes when the sheriff and the carrier come on stage; quite literally, Hal's words become good. He stops the sheriff, who is pursuing a "well known" man whom he "hath followed . . . unto this house" (2.4.506–10), by giving assurance, by giving his word:

> The man I do assure you is not here,
> For I myself at this time have employ'd him.
> And, sheriff, I will engage my word to thee
> That I will by to-morrow dinner-time
> Send him to answer thee.
>
> (2.4.512–16)

Here we see one instance of the credit through which Hal has paid Falstaff's part; Hal earns the credit by his aristocratic mastery of language. Hal's word is good because his speech is good. Shakespeare very deftly allows Hal's cadences to control the actions of others. Hal's gradual shift into blank verse seems to bring the sheriff up short, to catch him by surprise and to force him to measure out the contents of his inquiry. Hal greets the sheriff in slightly irregular pentameter:

> Now, Master Sheriff, what is your will with me?
>
> (506)

To which the sheriff responds in more regulated verse:

> First, pardon me, my lord. A hue and cry
> Hath followed certain men unto this house.
>
> (507–8)

Here Hal breaks the measure, interjecting his question—"What men?"(509)—which may mistakenly lead the sheriff and carrier to feel that, their inquiry having approached Hal's guilt, he has begun to let the measure of his language slip from his control. The sheriff, however, answers Hal in formal metre:

> One of them is well known, my gracious lord,
> A gross fat man.
>
> (2.4.510–11)

(He has avoided saying that another one of them also is well known—the prince himself.) The formality of his description of Falstaff gets debased by the carrier's irregular prose interjection: "As fat as butter" (511).

Ordinarily Hal would take the carrier's opening and respond in kind, with another metaphor about Falstaff's grossness. (At Coventry he, too, calls Falstaff "butter".) Instead, he responds in seven lines of formal, almost perfectly regular, pentameter, from which I have quoted above (The man I do assure you . . .") Hal completes his elegant passage by asking the sheriff to "Leave the house" (518), to which the sheriff humbly replies:

> I will, my lord. There are two gentlemen
> Have in this robbery lost three hundred marks.
>
> (2.4.519–20)

Hal of course must be informed of every point of the charge against the men the sheriff is seeking, but notice how the sheriff makes the active element of the charge the gentlemen who have "lost" the marks "in this robbery" and not the men who might have been said to have robbed the gentlemen. Hal's reply, however, takes on (or at least delegates to Falstaff) full active responsibility for robbing the men. In doing so, Hal, metrically, almost duplicates the sheriff's couplet, with the full stop occurring exactly at the same point:

> It may be so. If he have robb'd these men,
> He shall be answerable, and so farewell.
>
> (2.4.521–22)

The sheriff bids farewell to Hal with three iambs—"Good night, my noble lord" (523). This line of verse seems to ask to be completed by Hal with two more iambs or even dactyls, such as "Good night, sheriff." Instead, Hal responds with an independent line of pentameter:

> I think it is good morrow, is it not?
>
> (524)

Hal's response thoroughly surprises everyone, both because of its metrical independence from the context and because of the direct message it contains. By this one rather gracious line the prince suggests that he can step away from his environment—metrical, dramatic, and social—and initiate new patterns of control. Further, and more important, the prince has declared aloud—to the sheriff, to the audience, and to anyone lurking in the wings or backstage—that he can separate himself from the world of continuous revelry, the constant present of appetite, that he can discriminate among different times, and that he can use and discuss time as a process and, perhaps, as a force connected with history and responsibility. In short, Hal, at this crux in the drama, responds to Falstaff's question; he informs Falstaff and the sheriff that he knows the time of day.

We may assume that Hal's resolute control and his prescience take the sheriff aback ("Indeed, my lord, I think it be two a'clock," 525): Falstaff, however, "fast asleep behind the arras" (528), has missed Hal's performance, which may in part account for the rage, the overt death-wish, that, as M. D. Faber has noted, Hal expresses toward Falstaff when his sleeping and snorting body is revealed. The prince contrasts Falstaff's gluttony and indebtedness with his own implicit accumulation and, in keeping with the metaphor he had privately established earlier, in his soliloquy, with repayment of "the debt [he] never promised" (1.2.209). The debt, of course, works on two levels: "the money shall be paid back again with advantage" (2.4.547–48), but also the prince will go "to the court in the morning" (543–44), and they "must all to the wars" (544). He (they all?) will redeem Hal's dissolute life in the tavern by serving the King in battle. Hal employs the debt metaphor again during his greatest trial in battle; as he saves his father's life, he claims that he, as Prince of Wales, if perhaps not as Hal of Eastcheap, "never promiseth but he means to pay." After Hal has made good his promise, the King commends him: "Thou has *redeem'd* thy lost opinion, / And show'd thou mak'st *some tender* of my life" (5.4.43, 48–49). Hal prepares himself to pay back with his body his indebtedness to a force outside of his body, a force that, during the battle at Shrewsbury, comes to be represented by the body, or the life within the body, of his father, the king. This kind of indebtedness and compensation separates the Prince from Falstaff, who, as his "papers" show, remains indebted to the force of appetite, which of course has come to be represented by his own body. The differentiation between Hal and Falstaff degenerates into animosity, and further accounts for Hal's barely disguised aggression toward Falstaff ("I know this death will be a march of twelve score," 2.4.546–47).

Differentiation becomes animosity because Falstaff functions as Hal's antagonist as well as his "foil," although Hal does not make that discovery until the particular convergence of the events that the sheriff's arrival precipitated. Hal's conscious control of the present through the metrical dominance of the dialogue, his forthright public declaration that he knows the time, followed by his exposé of Falstaff's complete indifference to debts, time, and the state, dramatize, in a way that the rhetoric of Hal's initial soliloquy cannot, the separation between Hal's consciousness of his environment and Falstaff's enclosure within the needs and boundaries of his ego. But Hal does not experience this separation as an absolute opposition. The prince associates himself with Falstaffian egoism as part of what he considers a temporary denial and a period of austerity, but Hal uses this association with another's indulgences in order eventually to extend greatly his capacity for action within history, for satisfaction of his greater Machiavellian appetite for political power within the realm.

Prince Hal's Joke

David Sundelson

We have learned to distinguish at least three different Hals in *1 Henry IV*: "the most comparative, rascalliest, sweet young prince" (1.2.79–80) of the tavern (or at least of Falstaff's wishful fantasies); the heroic warrior who defeats Hotspur on the battlefield; and the Machiavel who hides the second figure beneath the first, who engineers the startling metamorphosis of "sweet wag" (1.2.23) into Prince of Wales. None of these three, however, is the Hal who executes with Poins a practical joke at the expense of the tavern waiter who gives him a bit of sugar as a token of friendship: "But, Ned, to drive away the time till Falstaff come, I prithee do thou stand in some byroom while I question my puny drawer to what end he gave me the sugar; and do thou never leave calling 'Francis!' that his tale to me may be nothing but 'Anon!' " (2.4.27–32). The game baffles Francis completely and seems out of character for "the king of courtesy" (2.4.10) who has just been drinking with the tavern's humblest customers as if he considered them his equals. A 1979 production at Stratford, Ontario, squeezed some laughter from the scene by giving Francis a hilariously exaggerated Cockney accent, but the joke itself is not inherently funny. Poins asks for an explanation that Hal never provides, and an audience is likely to share his perplexity. The episode at first glance seems both unpleasant and pointless: Hal teases Francis with special attention and the hope of "a thousand pound" (2.4.61) in exchange for his pennyworth of sugar, and then replaces the fairy-tale with a petty humiliation.

From *Shakespeare's Restoration of the Father.* © 1983 by Rutgers, The State University. Rutgers University Press, 1983.

The demonstration of mastery may be unpleasant, but it is not pointless for Hal or for us. What suggests the joke to him in the first place is the limited language of his drinking companion, "one that never spake other English in his life then 'Eight shillings and sixpence,' and 'You are welcome,' with this shrill addition, 'Anon, anon, Sir! Score a pint of bastard in the Half-moon' " (2.4.23–27). This minimal vocabulary makes Francis an extreme case of a common problem. Most obvious among the verbally handicapped in the play are Mortimer and his wife—"This is the deadly spite that angers me— / My wife can speak no English, I no Welsh" (3.1.186–87)—but Hotspur is scarcely better off. The military terms he pours out in his sleep are a sort of prattle without practice, useless when it comes to inspiring his troops:

> Better consider what you have to do
> Than I, that have not well the gift of tongue,
> Can lift your blood up with persuasion.
> (5.2.76–78)

Like Hotspur, Glendower and the king are great talkers but speak only a single isolating language.

Hal, on the other hand, masters not only the jargon of the drawers but his father's abstract, Latinate periods, the "princely tongue" (5.2.56) that lets him praise Hotspur "like a chronicle" (5.2.57), and the "unsavory similes" (1.2.78) and complex puns that make him Falstaff's match. Practical power in this play goes with the command of language and of rival fiction makers. Hal's joke anticipates his use of a "plain tale" (2.4.253) to deflate Falstaff's extravagant one and his victory in a battle which, as Hotspur puts it, "cuts me from my tale" (5.2.90). For an intoxicating moment, it gives him absolute supremacy, reducing Francis to "fewer words than a parrot" (2.4.98–99) while Hal himself bursts forth with manic abandon.

> FRANCIS: Anon, anon.
> PRINCE: Anon, Francis? No, Francis: but tomorrow,
>   Francis; or Francis, a Thursday; or indeed, Francis,
>   when thou wilt. But, Francis—
> FRANCIS: My lord?
> PRINCE: Wilt thou rob this leathern jerkin, crystal-button,
>   not-pated, agate-ring, puke-stocking,
>   caddis-garter, smooth-tongue, Spanish-pouch—.
>   (2.4.64–71)

The single word "anon" ("right away") which Francis cries out again and again points to another of the play's major concerns: time. This is a familiar topic in criticism, and I want to say only that Hal, himself intensely aware of time, turns Francis into the most ludicrous "time's fool" (5.4.81), to use Hotspur's phrase, of all those in the play subjected to its power, from the Carriers who must be up at four and on their way by sunrise to Hotspur himself.

The episode is thus one of "the small events that evoke a whole," but to explain Hal's peculiar euphoria and unkindness, we must consider another dimension. Boasting to Poins of his success with the common touch, Hal uses a family metaphor. "I have sounded the very bass—string of humility. Sirrah, I am sworn brother to a leash of drawers and can call them all by their christen names, as Tom, Dick, and Francis" (2.4.5–8). "Sworn brother" is in fact a dangerous category in a play where brotherhood, especially for Hal, creates rivalry more often than affection. We have seen that the king's dream of exchanging his own son for Hotspur makes the two rivals not only for preeminence in itself but for the king's approval and love. When Vernon describes Hal's challenge of Hotspur to single combat, he makes the connection between brotherhood and competition explicit.

> I never in my life
> Did hear a challenge urged more modestly,
> Unless a brother should a brother dare
> To manly exercise and proof of arms.
> (5.2.51–54)

Hal dramatizes the affectionate side of brotherhood by fraternizing with Francis and his kind. The hostility the relation generates also demands expression, however, and finds a vent in the practical joke. After creating a sworn brother, Hal triumphs over him effortlessly, and that triumph accounts for his considerable burst of pleasure. After sounding the bass-string of humility, he destroys any illusion of equality between himself and Francis, between the harried drawer and the dazzling prince.

Hal's evident delight in the game may also have another source: the predicament he imposes on the hapless Francis mirrors his own dilemma. It is a commonplace to say that Hal is torn by conflicting loyalties to the king and to Falstaff, to the father whose throne he will inherit and the "father ruffian" (2.4.449), as Hal calls him in this scene, who rules over the tavern. In the game, Hal can force someone else to experience in a small part the anxiety of trying to move in two directions at once, as the stage direction suggests: "The Drawer stands amazed, not knowing which way to go." Theater brings the illusion of control: Hal becomes the master of an anxiety instead of its victim.

However brief, such a victory has psychological value in a play where it is not mere metaphor to be pulled in two directions, where actual bodily disintegration is both a haunting fact and a recurrent fantasy. The opening speeches allude darkly if vaguely to "civil butchery" (1.1.13) and battlefield mutilation, the "beastly shameless transformation / By those Welshwomen done" (1.2.44–45) to Mortimer's soldiers. The body of England herself is in danger when Hotspur, Mortimer, and Glendower sit down with the map: "The Archdeacon hath divided it / Into three limits very equally" (3.1.69–70). Hotspur is equally reckless about his own body—"O, I could divide myself and go to buffets for moving such a dish of skim milk with so honorable an action" (2.3.31–33)—and Falstaff seems to answer him by proclaiming his physical integrity: "I am not a double man" (5.4.137).

The play's images of multiplication seem related to these threats of splitting, as the serpent's teeth in Ovid's tale, planted in the earth, spring up as "crowds of men at arms." Perhaps Falstaff's marvelous narrative of "Eleven buckram men grown out of two" (2.4.217–18) delights us as a magical reassurance that fission is a gain, not a loss, although the same can hardly be said of the dismaying proliferation of kings—"The King hath many marching in his coats" (5.3.25)—that confuses the rebels at the Battle of Shrewsbury. Hal will conquer Hotspur and Douglas by incorporating in himself those doubles of the king whom Douglas has killed: "The spirits / Of valiant Shirley, Stafford, Blunt, are in my arms" (5.4.40–41). His triumph over Francis anticipates that later victory.

> POINS: But hark ye; what cunning match have you
>   made with this jest of the drawer? Come, what's
>   the issue?
> PRINCE: I am now of all humors that have showed
>   themselves humors since the old days of goodman
>   Adam to the pupil age of this present twelve
>   o'clock at midnight.
>
>   (2.4.89–95)

Hal's psychological legacy from Richard II, the king his father deposed, is a crisis which Richard could articulate but not resolve: "Thus play I in one person many people, / And none contented"(5.5.3132). Here Hal transfers fears of fragmentation onto a scapegoat, or perhaps two of them since his description of the Vintner turns him into an incoherent assemblage of details ("agate-ring, puke-sticking," and so on), each one of them a compound in itself—a rhetorical version of fragments within fragments. At the same time, Hal celebrates himself as multiple but whole and potent—no small achievement for a prince of many faces, whatever private self he may eventually sacrifice to become the successful King Henry V.

That sacrifice becomes increasingly visible in the final scenes of this play, however. Personal change is not for Glendower, proud that no man "call [him] pupil" (3.1.44), or for Hotspur, and in certain ways Hal's is a sadder story. The prince who threatened to "prove a micher [truant], and eat blackberries" (2.4.404–5) has now, according to Vernon, "master'd . . . a double spirit / Of teaching and of learning" (5.2.63–64). But Shakespeare never lets us forget that Hal's education is both a gain and a loss; his new mastery seems to preclude not only blackberries but also the greater pleasure of authentically personal speech, the kind that erupts in the scene with Francis. Instead of the devastating parody of a rival who "kills me some six or seven dozen of Scots at a breakfast, washes his hands, and says to his wife, 'Fie upon this quiet life! I want work' " (2.4.102–5), we get self-assertion tempered by courtesy in the challenge to Hotspur that wins Vernon's approval. But by using Vernon to report it, Shakespeare reminds us that Hal's challenge is expert political theater, and the rest of his brotherly moments are just as stagy.

Before Shrewsbury, Hal's brother John has figured only as his replacement in Council; now, with the king as audience, Hal finds a new enthusiasm: "Before, I lov'd thee as a brother, John, / But now, I do respect thee with my soul" (5.4.19–20). Hal makes a grand gesture of allowing John to free the captured Douglas, but he can be generous at little cost to a rival whose dignity has been tarnished by his flight from battle, and he makes at best a rather patronizing brother to "this boy" (5.4.129–30). Brotherly ambivalence in Hotspur produces genuine passion, however disturbing, but Hal's stilted and cautious valediction to his chief rival is marked instead by a curious numbness.

> It thou wert sensible of courtesy,
> I should not make so dear a show of zeal
> But let my favors hide thy mangled face;
> And, even in thy behalf, I'll thank myself
> For doing these fair rites of tenderness.
> (5.4.94–98)

Self-consciousness dominates the farewell, not grief or recognition. Hal can express tenderness only toward a face that is mangled, and even then—"I'll thank myself"—the gesture seems ambiguous and solipsistic. Hal will be a king whose subjects take him for a comrade, but true brotherhood is only for men who will not wear a crown.

Henry IV: Prince Hal and Falstaff

A. D. Nuttall

I have said [elsewhere] that Shakespeare likes to take a stereotype and then work against it. The stereotype of Prince Hal in relation to his father, Henry IV, is that of the uncontrolled young man, sowing his wild oats, in rebellion against an authoritarian father. Shakespeare has no sooner set this up for us than he begins to undermine it.

First, he contrives a dramatic echo-chamber, by giving Hal a secondary father. His name is Falstaff. W. H. Auden observes [in *The Dyer's Hand*] that, if you look at Hal's associates, they are really rather odd. What sort of people would one expect to find in company with a prince out on the tiles? Every generation has its own word for the answer to this question: Corinthians, rakes, bucks, blades, *jeunesse dorée,* mashers, Bright Young Things, the Beautiful People. These are not what we find about Hal. Admittedly there is one who is certainly smooth and may be young, Poins, but thereafter the stage is engrossed by an extraordinary collection of aged and seedy persons: an obese alcoholic of advanced years, various strutting scarecrows from that strange Elizabethan underworld of discharged officers and decayed soldiers, and some superannuated prostitutes. Why?

The best answer (the reader may be surprised to find me granting this] is not one resting on psychological probability. It is thematic, It is Falstaff that Shakespeare needs and all the rest is a sort of moving cloud of circumambient Falstaffiana. Shakespeare needs him first of all, as I have suggested, as a parody-father. We saw how in *Othello* Shakespeare made use of an

---

From *A New Mimesis: Shakespeare and the Representation of Reality.* © 1983 by A. D. Nuttall. Methuen, 1983.

immediate, visual contrast to enforce the theme of the outsider—the black Othello among the shining Venetians. So here (though it is somewhat less obvious) he needs a visual tableau: a grey-haired, physically disgraced old man and a superb youngster. They should *look*, for a moment, like father and son. The point is underlined in the famous scene in which Falstaff plays the part of King Henry admonishing his errant son (*1 Henry IV*, 2.4.418–64). Here we are formally presented with the required tableau.

It does not reinforce but definitely and immediately reverses the stereotype. Instead of the stern father and the 'dropout' son, we have the exact opposite. The jaded slang of the 1960s may bring out the paradox. Falstaff is an aged hippy (fundamentally uncontrolled, given over to the pleasure principle, certainly a dropout from practical society, with his own drug—alcohol—and his own lyrical mode of speech, contemptuous of legal and other convention); meanwhile Hal, we gradually learn, is a rigidly controlled personality, dedicated to effective government and the subordination of personal pleasure to legal and political ends.

At the end of 1.2, in *Part 1*, Prince Hal is left alone on the stage, and pronounces his famous explanatory soliloquy.

> I know you all, and will a while uphold
> The unyok'd humour of your idleness;
> Yet herein will I imitate the sun,
> Who doth permit the base contagious clouds
> To smother up his beauty from the world,
> That, when he please again to be himself,
> Being wanted, he may be more wond'red at
> By breaking through the foul and ugly mists
> Of vapours that did seem to strangle him.
> If all the year were playing holidays,
> To sport would be as tedious as to work;
> But when they seldom come, they wish'd for come;
> And nothing pleaseth but rare accidents.
> So, when this loose behaviour I throw off
> And pay the debt I never promised,
> By how much better than my word I am,
> By so much shall I falsify men's hopes;
> And, like bright metal on a sullen ground,
> My reformation, glitt'ring o'er my fault,
> Shall show more goodly and attract more eyes
> Than that which hath no foil to set it off.

> I'll so offend to make offence a skill,
> Redeeming time when men think least I will.
> (1.2.188–210)

Is the prince making cold-blooded political use of the people who suppose him to be their friend? This is the kind of speech which Levin Schücking (*Character Problems in Shakespeare's Plays*) held up to show the primitive dramatic technique of Shakespeare; it is not naturalistic, for in naturalistic drama we are encouraged to notice not only the content of the speech but also its manner, so that when, say, Leontes tells us in *The Winter's Tale* that he knows his wife is unchaste we infer from his distracted manner that his judgement is awry. But with speeches of "direct self-explanation," such as Hal's, Schücking suggests that any such inference is out of place. They are a spoken equivalent of the programme note. The actor, though he continues to say "I" rather than "he," in effect doffs his role and comes forward to explain things to the audience. Thus the object of the prince's speech is reassurance: "Do not be anxious about this young man; he is going to be a great king in due course."

With regard to the present speech this view seems to me substantially correct. It is not of course the direct address to the audience as mankind which we find in medieval drama; nor is it the "logical joke" type of audience reference common in the Renaissance theatre. Shakespeare has the prince stand watching the retreating backs of those he has just been joking with and, once they are securely out of earshot, address them in terms which (within the drama) are intended rather to articulate his own thoughts than have any effect on them. Formally (if that is the kind of criticism we are to engage in) the speech is not a direct address to the audience but an apostrophic soliloquy (that is, a soliloquy which is formally, but only formally, addressed to another person). But, at the same time, such soliloquies are formally distinct from the dramatic texture of the rest, and the extra-mimetic function of reassurance is quite inescapable. Even if the actor may begin in a fairly naturalistic manner—musingly—the speech rapidly gathers formal momentum, and the element of *virtual* address to the audience grows stronger.

But it by no means follows from any of this that the speech has ceased to be mimetic. It is a rule of explanatory soliloquy that we should attend strictly to content. Very well, let us do that.

Implicit in the formal account has been a suggestion that any feeling of shock we may have felt at the prince's cold manipulation of people is removed if we refuse to infer character and restrict ourselves to information.

But this speech does not say, "Though I am now keeping vile company, all will be well, since a sudden change will come over me, and the surprise which this will create will be wholly salutary for the realm and the crown." What is makes utterly clear is that Hal himself proposes to bring about this transformation deliberately. The disquieting element of cool manipulation is not something we infer from a naturalistic interpretation of Hal's manner, it is something we are told. If the speech is self-explanation and provides the audience with information, this is part of the information it provides. Everything, to be sure, depends on the meaning of the word "that" in the following lines:

> Yet herein will I imitate the sun,
> Who doth permit the base contagious clouds
> To smother up his beauty from the world
> That, when he please again to be himself,
> Being wanted, he may be more wond'red at
> By breaking through the foul and ugly mists.
> (1.2.190–95)

The word "that," in this context, undoubtedly means "in order that."

This insistence on an uncomfortably intrusive purposive particle where we might have expected a more neutral grammar of mere consequence is precisely what led, in the final speculation of our last section, to the "existentialist" Iago. The distance between Prince Hal and Iago is great but not, perhaps, unbridgeable. W. H. Auden (the presiding genius of this part of the book) noted a curious similarity between this speech by the prince and one of Iago's soliloquies, similarly placed, early in the play:

> For when my outward action doth demonstrate
> The native act and figure of my heart
> In compliment extern, 'tis not long after
> But I will wear my heart upon my sleeve
> For daws to peck at: I am not what I am.
> (*Othello* 1.1.62–66)

Both passages are Machiavellian in style; that is, they evoke an ethos of devious cunning. This also works against the critic who believes that a formalist reading can dispel all distaste. It is an inference from the manner, but not a naturalistic inference; it is a formal one.

Let us confess that this is a strange speech, marked by a very considerable tension. Shakespeare adopts a "naïve" technique, but he does so with a complex sense of context and for a particular effect. The actor who allows the text to speak in him will find that he gradually freezes as the speech proceeds. The director who understands this process may ensure that a strong light falls on the actor's almost unmoving face, on the line, "Herein will I imitate the sun." The sun is the emblem of royalty. The office of the king may thus momentarily shine through the actor figurally, and become a felt presence on the stage.

But, when every concession has been made, the speech is not naturalistic; forms are at work which are not the transparent forms of realism; the speech purveys information rather than betraying an attitude: the result is that we find ourselves presented with an essentially mimetic statement about the *character* of Prince Hal. The presumption of twentieth-century criticism—that choric exegesis precludes characterization—is shattered when the choric information turns out itself to be, baldly and explicitly, information about character. It is never good practice with Shakespeare to ignore or repress worrying, initially unwanted complexities. Far better to assimilate them, to imagine and to think. When one is watching or reading Shakespeare, this thinking can be done almost subliminally, with a wise passiveness. When criticizing or interpreting Shakespeare, one must think explicitly.

The speech certainly contained great comfort for the Tudor audience, but it is a comfort shot through with unease. There is nothing unhistorical in the supposition that an Elizabethan could have been repelled by manipulation of people's affections. The Machiavellian "twinge" in the style is not there by chance. But (and here a Tudor would have been more perceptive than a modern audience) it is all directed to the good end of stable government. And so Prince Hal is a White Machiavel. This powerful moment of confession which is also a self-dedication and a kind of promise precedes and sets the dominant tone for what follows. It is not wiped out by Warwick's observing in *Part 2* at 4.4.68–72 (long after our conception has formed) that the prince kept low company to educate himself in the moral variety of his people.

Falstaff, who is all intelligence, knows everything about the prince except this, his chilling, profoundly moral, private plan. Nevertheless, Shakespeare illogically permits two episodes in which Falstaff learns the truth. One of them is the celebrated rejection of Falstaff by the new-made King Henry V, but that poses no problem of consistency in Falstaff because it comes at the end. The more problematic one occurs in the tableau scene with which we began, where Falstaff plays the part of the prince's father (*1 Henry IV*, 2.4). When Falstaff has had his turn, the game is reversed, Hal plays his father and Falstaff plays the prince. The fun is uproarious but through it we begin to sense a profound collision and awakening. Falstaff finds that he is pleading for the prince's love and, at the second when he discovers he can never have it, is interrupted by a loud banging on the door; breathless figures with urgent news come blundering *across* the duel between Hal and Falstaff—now at last explicit. So the moment is seen, once, in total clarity, and them muffled in extraneous noise.

PRINCE: . . . wherein worthy, but in nothing?

FALSTAFF: I would your Grace would take me with you;
    whom means your Grace?

PRINCE: That villainous, abominable misleader of youth,
    Falstaff, that old white-bearded Satan.

FALSTAFF: My lord, the man I know.

PRINCE: I know thou dost.

FALSTAFF: But to say I know more harm in him than in myself
    were to say more than I know. That he is old—the more
    the pity—his white hairs do witness it; but that he is,
    saving your reverence—a whoremaster, that I utterly
    deny. If sack and sugar be a fault, God help the wicked!
    If to be old and merry be a sin, then many an old host
    that I know is damn'd; if to be fat be to be hated, then
    Pharaoh's lean kine are to be loved. No, my good lord:
    banish Peto, banish Bardolph, banish Poins; but, for
    sweet Jack Falstaff, kind Jack Falstaff, valiant Jack
    Falstaff—and therefore more valiant, being, as he is, old
    Jack Falstaff—banish not him thy Harry's company,
    banish not him thy Harry's company. Banish plump Jack,
    and banish all the world.

PRINCE: I do, I will.   [*A knocking heard*]
        [*Re-enter* BARDOLPH, *running*]

BARDOLPH: O, my lord, my lord! the sheriff with a most
    monstrous watch is at the door.

FALSTAFF: Out, ye rogue! Play out the play: I have much to
    say in the behalf of Falstaff.
               [*Re-enter the* HOSTESS]

HOSTESS: O Jesu, my lord, my lord!

PRINCE: Heigh, heigh! the devil rides upon a fiddlestick; what's
    the matter?

HOSTESS: The sheriff and all the watch are at the door; they are
    come to search the house. Shall I let them in?

FALSTAFF: Dost thou hear, Hal? Never call a true piece of gold a counterfeit. Thou art essentially mad, without seeming so.

(1 Henry IV 2.4.443–76)

Notice in this exchange how at one point a laugh is killed, or at least checked. "Valiant Jack Falstaff" raises the laugh but "old Jack Falstaff" silences it with truth. When the prince answers, from a masklike face, "I do, I will," the secret is out.

When I quoted Falstaff's words flung desperately across the violent interruption, I made use of an emendation. The First and Second Folios and the string of Quarto editions (the fifth of which was probably the copy-text for the First Folio) all give "made" where I have given "mad" at 2.4.476. The word "mad" is an emendation, but is pretty well the smallest emendation possible. This becomes clear if we imagine the passage written in an Elizabethan hand. Shakespeare almost certainly wrote a secretary hand, in which case the words might have looked something like this:

In this hand *d* is written 𝒹 and *e* is written backwards as 𝒩. The *d* is a little taller, may have a closed loop at the bottom and a large loop at the top, but it is undoubtedly very like an *e* and in actual specimens of secretary hand the two letters are sometimes quite indistinguishable: you can tell which is which only by context.

Let us suppose that Shakespeare wanted to write the word "mad," spelling it, as he may well have done, with two *d*'s. It might then look like this.

madd

And of course this can be read as "made." Indeed it says "made," taken letter by letter, just as much as it says "madd."

All of this would become a good deal weaker if we knew that Shakespeare strongly distinguished his *d*'s and his *e*'s and avoided spellings like "madd." We have no conclusive evidence on this point, but such evidence as we possess points the other way. The only specimen of handwriting, apart from some signatures, which has a good chance of being Shakespeare's is to be found on three pages of the manuscript "Book of Sir Thomas

More," the passage written in what is usually called "Hand D." This passage is one of several "additions" to the text by revisers. The word *mad* does not occur on any of these three pages, but a great deal of doubling of letters does occur. The writing of Hand D spells "got" with two *t*'s, "sit" with two *t*'s, "sin" with two *n*'s, cut with two *t*'s and "dogs" with two *g*'s. Such a man, one feels, would scarcely flinch from "mad" with two *d*'s. Moreover, several of the *d*'s in the manuscript are identical in form with the *e*'s; for example, in the upper half of Folio 9, the *d* of "God" in the first line is like the *e* of "power" in the fourth line; the *d* of "hands" (thirteenth line) is like the *e* of "kneels" (sixteenth line). The graph is very close all the time.

It might be thought that, given the fact that "made" and "mad" are common words, Shakespeare's supposed manner of writing and spelling should have led to frequent textual confusion. In fact, however, although both words are common they are very different in force and meaning; as a result context usually precludes confusion. But, for all that, there are several cases in the text of Shakespeare of possible confusion of these forms; for example, in *The Winter's Tale*, at 3.3.115, the Clown says, in the Folio, "You are a mad old man" but most modern editors accept Theobald's substitution of "made." The 1609 Quarto of Sonnet 79, "Expense of spirit in a waste of shame," gave "made in pursuit" for line 9.

Given all this it is very nearly a question of printing the reading one prefers. The Folio editors in the seventeenth century made no bones about it. It would seem that as soon as they spotted "made" they changed it to "mad." The New Arden editor in our own century was obviously tempted to do the same thing but drew back because he felt "mad" gave a difficult or impossible sense. Does it? "Essentially made"—now that is really difficult. The phrase is explained as a continuation of the previous talk about true gold and counterfeiting, and "essentially made" is supposed to mean "made of true gold." The suggestion is highly implausible. It is not Shakespearean English (or any other). No parallel usage, as far as I know, has ever been shown for *essentially* in this sense. But "essentially mad" on the other hand is obviously good Shakespearean English. Does not Hamlet say, "I essentially am not in madness, / But mad in craft" (*Hamlet*, 3.4.187–88)? The sense "mad" in this passage is both clear and powerful. Falstaff has seen that the prince does not have any friends at all and he, the semiprofessional fool, suddenly cries out, "Why, you're the crazy one; You don't look it, but you are!" Hal is inside out. Instead of concealing his human features beneath a stiff, impersonal mask, he wears the golden mask of kingship beneath an ordinary, smiling human face.

Thus the stereotype of wild son and authoritarian father is reversed. Falstaff is that other kind of archetypal old man who derives by a kind of creative misreading from Paul's *vetus homo,* the old man we must put off in order to put on the new; the old Adam, the unregenerate, the happy inhabitant of a fallen world which remains, if not Eden-like, then Arcadian, excluded from the New Jerusalem. Falstaff says, "Dost thou hear, Hal? Thou knowest in the state of innocency Adam fell; and what should poor Jack Falstaff do in the days of villainy? Thus seest I have more flesh than another man, and therefore more frailty" (*1 Henry IV* 3.3.164–67). Paul calls the old Adam "the body of Sin," an expression which immediately and naturally invites joyous elaboration from Falstaff. But what now of Hal's father? Surely there the stereotype is straightforwardly maintained?

In fact, it is not. We learn this largely from the parodic structure of the play. Falstaff cannot be a figure of authority because he is a criminal. But what if the king is himself a criminal? This is a subversive idea, and there is no doubt that it is present in the plays. The dubiety of the king's right to rule is fundamental. The prince knows that it is dubious and all his dedication hinges of the decision that it is better to maintain a usurpation than to let the realm slip into anarchy.

There is a certain sort of learned critic who loves to point out that Falstaff must be classified as an evil force, since he stands for drink, conviviality and pleasure and has no sense of his responsibility to the great cause, the putting down of rebellion. All this depends, perhaps, on the authenticity and rightness of the order which is being maintained. But these same learned critics come at length in their dogged progress upon the fact that the king's rule is inauthentic. The rebels are not more rebellious then the king himself. The effect of this is to reopen the ethical debate about Falstaff. Dr Johnson was right when he reminded the reader—who, be it noted, he assumed all those years ago, would be distressed at the departure of Falstaff—that Falstaff utters no single "sentiment of generosity" in the course of the plays. Yet Auden can see Falstaff as a parabolic figure of charity. How is this?

It is partly an effect of style. Falstaff speaks a golden Shakespearean English which makes him the centre of a small world of joy wherever he goes. Above all, in the very jaws of senility and death, he is life, and whenever he comes near there is a real danger that the great warlords will be seen for what they perhaps are—mere bloody men, agents of death.

Yet (with Falstaff one has to go on and on saying "yet" since he is "poem unlimited"), even while Falstaff impugns the practical mystique of the ruler, he is made the great expression in the plays of what we may call the impractical mystique. Falstaff, who cannot get on with live King Henry, is on the best of terms with dead King Arthur. If a sense of England as a ruined Arcadia or Eden survives at all in *Henry IV* it is because of Falstaff. This comes partly from the language of the Falstaff scenes with its preference for immemorial, rustic ways of measuring time—"I have known thee these twenty-nine years, come peascodtime" (*2 Henry IV* 2.4.368–70). There is a speech in *As You Like It* which brings Falstaff to mind, and it is possible to piece together why this is so. Charles says to Oliver,

> They say he is already in the Forest of Arden, and a many merry men with him; and there they live like the old Robin Hood of England. They say many young gentlemen flock to him every day, and fleet the time carelessly, as they did in the golden world.
>
> (*As You Like It* 1.1.105–9)

Falstaff says in his first scene, "Let us be Diana's foresters, gentlemen of the shade, minions of the moon" (*1 Henry IV* 1.2.25–25). Falstaff might almost be describing that band of Kentish poachers who stole deer from Penshurst park after blacking their faces and calling themselves the servants of the Queen of the Fairies. But notice that in Falstaff's speech we have, as in Charles's speech, the forest and the gentlemen—surely merry ones, too. Then in *Part 3* Piston speaks of "golden times" (5.3.95) and Silence sings in a quavering voice of Robin Hood (5.3.102). And so the elements of the *As You Like It* speech are resembled.

Then there is the trail of references to King Arthur (king over the lost England). These are of increasing power. In *Part 2* at 2.4, Falstaff enters singing, "When Arthur first in court" (2.4.33) and then breaks off with a request to Francis to empty the jordan. Then in the great pastoral-comical-elegiacal scene, 3.2, Shallow says that long ago he was Sir Dagonet in Arthur's show (3.2.273). Since, according to Malory, Dagonet was Arthur's fool and Shallow here plays fool to Falstaff the effect of the allusion is to turn Falstaff for a second into a grey echo of Arthur himself. But the best comes in *Henry V*. There Pistol, the Hostess, Nym, Bardolph and the Boy are talking about the way Falstaff died and wondering whether his soul is in hell or heaven. Bardolph cries out, "Would I were with him, wheresome'er he is, either in heaven or in hell!" But the Hostess answers,

> Nay, sure, he's not in hell: he's in Arthur's bosom, if ever man went to Arthur's bosom. 'A made a finer end, and went away an it had been any christom child; 'a parted even just between twelve and one, ev'n at the turning o' th' tide.
>
> (*Henry V* 2.3.7–14)

Comic malapropism can be eagerly powerful. The Hostess has confused the story in Like about Dives and Lazarus with the story of Arthur. To that most potent story she has joined the story Luke tells of the poor leper who was shut out from the rich man's gate, as Falstaff was shut out from the presence of Hal, and how the poor man was after death raised up to Abraham's bosom while the rich man was left in hell (is there anyone left who can believe that Shakespeare was unequivocally against Falstaff when the imagery can do things like that?). To that scriptural story the Hostess has joined the legend of the old king who lies sleeping under Snowdon or perhaps Glastonbury Tor till we need him again.

Thus the anti–father. But, as I have suggested, the prince's relation with his real father is likewise, though less obviously, subversive of the stereotype. Once again it is the old man who is the outlaw and the son is the possible agent of control. The old man looks hungrily to his son for an authority he could never attain himself. One could imagine various possible reactions in a son faced with such a father, such a kingdom: a despairing withdrawal from political life, an equally desperate ferocity. Hal falls into neither of these. Instead, he commits himself, body and soul to confirming, both morally and by force of arms, the power of the crown. He knows that he is more completely alone than anyone else, more, even, than his father. His situation requires of him more perhaps than should be asked of anyone. It requires him to extinguish his humanity in the interests of the realm. E. M. Forster once wrote that if ever he was in a position where he was forced to choose between his country and his friend he hoped he would have the guts to choose his friend. People respond warmly to the passage, but I suspect that they do so because betraying one's country is a remote abstraction to most of us. Whether or not the cause is just, whether the realm is holy or corrupt, treachery on the part of the king must mean suffering, on a horrible scale. As Angelo, the fallen archangel of *Measure for Measure*, said, the good man in office must learn to pity people he does not know, has never seen (2.2.101).

Hal's White Machiavellian speech in which he explains his strange purpose produces, in the author of this book, a distinct physical symptom, a tightening at the back of the throat. The same symptom is produced in the same subject by Sonnet 94:

> They that have power to hurt and will do none,
> That do not do the thing they most do show,
> Who, moving others, are themselves as stone,
> Unmoved, cold, and to temptation slow—

> They rightly do inherit Heaven's graces,
> And husband nature's riches from expense;
> They are the lords and owners of their faces,
> Others but stewards of their excellence.

This seems to be one of the sonnets addressed to the Friend, the young, beautiful man whom Shakespeare loves and whose unresponsiveness is seen by Shakespeare at one moment as a kind of blasphemy and at others—by an immense effort of will—as admirable.

If this were the nineteenth century I should now be permitted to speculate—to wonder whether Prince Hal was not founded on the beloved Friend, whether our difficulties with the prince may not arise from the fact that we, unlike Shakespeare, are not in love with him, so that for us he gives light but not warmth, to wonder whether the rejected Falstaff, the myriad-minded, the genius with words, the messy, disordered man, might not be an ectype of Shakespeare himself, who in this sonnet made an intense effort to give praise to the other sort, to the beautiful, reserved man. Such speculations, though untestable, are not fundamentally irrational.

It may be said that the public mimesis of possible realities is one thing, and the dark genesis of a work in the private affections of the poet another, but reality is a turbulent ocean which endlessly overflows dykes and breakwaters of this kind; the terms for interpreting even an ostentatious fictitious profession of love are modified by our sense of its source; we may strive to restrict "source" to fictional "persona" but the restriction is artificial, requires an unsleeping vigilance to enforce it; left to themselves the most literate, the most literary readers of *The Waste Land* will sense, behind the epicene Tiresias, the learned and quizzical American poet. But, for all that, the inferences have become unmanageable. It is better to stick to what we can see; and we can see a little (I am still trying to understand the tightening at the back of the throat).

The phrase "lords and owners of their faces" objectively recalls the prince, for the *face* is associated with royalty from Richard II smashing the looking glass to the almost surrealist speech in *Henry V* where Hal, now the king, imagines his features turning to unfeeling stone (3.1.11–14). Moreover, the preservative coldness of the Friend strongly resembles Hal's—he too husbands England's riches from expense. But the sonnet ends in a barely controlled revulsion of feeling which is not, as far as I can see anywhere reflected in the dramatic sequence from *Part 1* of *Henry IV* to *Henry V*.

In Prince Hal, Shakespeare gives us a mode of goodness which is embarrassing. The man is attractive but behind his easy manner lies something very unattractive and it is that unattractive something which is most deeply, most uncomfortably involved with real virtue. But the prince is not quite a saint and the conflict of humanity and dedication can make a fool of him (where people like Hotspur and Falstaff, oddly enough, are secure). In *Part 2,* at 4.5, the old king lies dying in the Palace of Westminster. There has been talk of Prince Hal, his way of life, of the fact that at this of all times no one knows where he is. Then Westmoreland comes with good news: the rebellion is over. The king cries out, "O Westmoreland, thou art a summer bird, / Which ever in the haunch of Winter sings / The lifting up of day" (4.4.91–3). But the shock of the good news is too great and now he is conveyed to the inner room. The crown is placed beside him. Then, out of step and out of time, the prince suddenly enters, talking in too loud a voice, for which he is politely rebuked by Warwick. The prince moderates his voice and says that he will sit beside the now sleeping king. The rest withdraw and the prince's eyes fall on the crown: "O polish'd perturbation! golden care!" (4.5.23). Then his eye strays to a downy feather which has settled by the mouth and nostrils of the king; it lies there, unmoving, and the prince is suddenly sure that his father is dead:

> My Gracious lord! my father!
> This sleep is sound indeed; this is a sleep
> That from this golden rigol hath divorc'd
> So many English Kings. Thy due from me
> Is tears and heavy sorrows of the blood
> Which nature, love and filial tenderness,
> Shall, O dear father, pay thee plenteously.
> My due from thee is this imperial crown,
> Which, as immediate from thy place and blood,
> Derives itself to me [*Putting on the crown*]
> > Lo where it sits—
> Which God shall guard; and put the world's whole strength
> Into one giant arm, it shall not force
> This lineal honour from me. This from thee
> Will I to mine leave as tis left to me.
>
> > (4.5.34–47)

But the king is not dead. Again he revives, to find himself alone. He calls for Warwick and the rest. Where is the prince? And then, a moment later, "*Where is the crown?*"—"Is he so hasty that he doth suppose / My sleep my death?" (4.5.61–62). Then Warwick returns to say that he found the prince weeping in the next room and that he is coming at once. The prince enters and the king orders all the rest to leave. Hal speaks first:

> I never thought to hear you speak again.
> (4.5.92)

The king's answer is savage:

> Thy wish was father, Harry, to that thought.
> I stay too long by thee, I weary thee.

At last the prince is allowed to make his excuses, to explain what he has done. This he performs brilliantly and touches his father's heart:

>   There is your crown,
> And He that wears the crown immortally
> Long guard it yours! (*Kneeling*) If I affect it more
> Than as your honour and as your renown,
> Let me no more from this obedience rise. . . .
> Coming to look on you, thinking you dead—
> And dead almost, my liege, to think you were—
> I spake unto this crown, as having sense,
> And thus upbraided it: "The care on thee
>   depending
> Hath fed upon the body of my father;
> Therefore thou best of gold art worst of gold. . . ."
>   Thus, my most royal liege,
> Accusing it, I put it on my head,
> To try with it—as with an enemy
> That had before my face murd'red my father—.

The king is won by the speech and calls his son to sit by him on the bed. This is the part which, above all, produces the constriction in the throat. For the most terrible thing about this scene is that the prince, in the most venial way, lies. He did not address the crown as an enemy, nor was it in that spirit that he took up the crown in his hands. Shakespeare, I think, does not want us to make any mistake about this, for he shows us the two things in succession, first the taking up of the crown and then the prince's account, given under pressure. We know that when the prince thought his father dead he experienced two great emotions one after the other; first real (and immense) grief for his father, and then a quite different feeling: "Now it has come; now I am the King." In the story which he tells his father he changes things, so that his thoughts are of Henry throughout.

Yet we can hardly say that we have "seen through" Hal, discovered the cold ambition that lies beneath. Shakespeare refuses to make it so easy for us. What we have seen and what the prince had dissembled is, precisely, not ambition, but dedication. This is merely the worst of his ordeals. There is indeed a fierce irony in the fact that this was the prince with the common tough, the ease manner with all sorts and conditions, for no character in Shakespeare, except perhaps Iago, is so utterly alone.

The scene between the prince and his father is very like that other great and complex scene, written about a year afterwards: the quarrel scene in *Julius Caesar* with its double version of the death of Portia. Henry dies, lives and dies again and so, in a manner, does Portia (though outside the scene). The sense of anguished back-tracking over what was said only moments before ("I said an elder soldier, not a better. / Did I say better?" *Julius Caesar* 4.3.56–57) is common to both. Strongest of all is the sense in both scenes of a good man, in a state of near disintegration, exerting all his skills, all his *art*, to prevent horror and chaos from taking over, and the audience being made, in a way which is almost unseemly, privy both to the mendacity (almost invisible with Hal, palpable with Brutus) and to the heroic effort of moral will. Both Brutus and the prince are in a manner made fools of, yet in either case the phrase "made fools of" is too coarse for the work it needs to do. Cassius's comment, extraordinary in its combination of affectionate admiration, charity and analytic intelligence,

> I have as much of this in art as you,
> But yet my nature could not bear it so.
> (*Julius Caesar* 4.3.192–93)

corresponds to the king's answer to the prince, loving yet somehow finding space within that love to register the *rhetorical* skill of what the prince has just done:

> O my son,
> God put it in thy mind to take it hence
> That thou might'st win the more thy father's love,
> Pleading so wisely in excuse of it!
> (*2 Henry IV* 4.5.178–81)

Both scenes show us more than we are accustomed to receive. Both force on us the radical opposition of nature and art in a manner which will not permit the resolution of the "nature" half of the opposition into further covert rules of art (which is what formalist critics allege). Instead the dramatist turns the tables by reminding us that art is actually employed *in* life, by Stoic commanders or anointed princes, when life is most itself, most amorphous, most crushing. The fact that a playwright has contrived the whole impression by means of fictions in no way abolishes this point. For his fiction is unintelligible unless we permit ourselves the (wholly natural) recourse to real human behaviour. The element of recalcitrant "mere probability" is so strong in these scenes that it is not only conventions of Elizabethan drama which are subtly contested. Our own comforting conventions, in which we codify our admiration of the good and our contempt for the bad, are themselves contested, so that people do not care to say, even to themselves, that Brutus, or Prince Hal lied. More often than not the thought has actually been repressed before the spectator has left the theatre. Is it not that the mirror of nature shows us spectacular blemishes (these can be accommodated, neutralized and then enjoyed by way of an appropriate rhetoric). Shakespeare shows us the painful enmeshing of falsity with good feeling as it actually happens. The scenes, from every formal point of view, are chaotic. But they have a glaringly obvious, single, clarifying source in reality itself.

Prince Hal is a late-born man, delivered over to a world which has lost its freshness. His father obtained his crown by deposing Richard II. Richard, though in many ways a fairly repellent person, was the true, anointed king, God's regent upon earth. This fact alone has power to irradiate the England of the play, *Richard II*. The dying Gaunt rebukes the king for his betrayal of the realm, yet throughout his famous speech (2.1.31–66), except for a single phrase, the praise of England remains in the present tense. The England of the usurper, Henry, lacking its point of intersection with the divine order, is greyer, less definite, less heraldic. War is seen less in terms of its high intelligible crises and more in terms of sheer mess—"bloody noses and crack'd crowns." "I never did see such pitiful rascals . . . Tut, tut; good enough to toss; food for powder, food for powder; they'll fill a pit as well as better: tush, man, mortal men, mortal men." "There's not three of my hundred and fifty left alive, and they are for the town's end, to beg during life" (*Part 1* 2.3.90; 4.2.62f; 5.3.36f).

Part 1 of *Henry IV* opens with an overwhelming impression of weariness, of more to do than can be done—"So shaken as we are, so wan with care. . . ." *Richard II* was about the fall of a king, but it was a true king that fell, and this gives the drama a unified and spectacular tragic structure. With the two loosely joined parts of *Henry IV* we get a cooler dramatic technique, inclining more to piecemeal exploration and an agnostic pluralism. In both *Richard II* and *Henry IV,* we find scenes of mediation on the idea of England as a ruined garden but they are very different. In *Richard II* we have a tiny, jewelled allegory, in which two unnamed gardeners, in measured verse, liken the conduct of a kingdom to their own simple art. All is structured, everywhere there is correspondence and analogy, all thoughts begun are concluded. But in *Henry IV* we have instead the Gloucestershire scenes, in which Falstaff, Shallow and —name of names—Master Silence ramble on together in the orchard of Shallow's decaying farm. These scenes are extremely naturalistic—almost Chekhovian—full of inconsequential remarks, voices trailing away into nothingness, of memories, mundane queries about such things as the present price of bullocks, of a sense of imminent death. In the absence of conclusive structures we are given an atmosphere, compounded of last year's apples, the grey heads of old men, of sweetness and barrenness, and of futility.

This is the non-kingdom which Hal is to inherit from his father. Somehow he must unify the kingdom, make the crown real again. This is the proper context of the strange speech of "direct self-explanation" with which we began. He has a mission (and there can be no doubt that it is a fully moral mission—unless the country is unified the blood and suffering will be endless). He dedicates himself utterly to the mission and, in its service, to a strange plan. He needs, on his inheritance, to seize the initiative, and for this he must be master of an element of spectacular surprise. In fact the people must be surprised (in the etymological sense of the word—"taken unawares") by majesty. But if majesty is to surprise it must be preceded by its opposite—ignominy, irresponsibility. And so the bizarre logic of the situation tells Hal that he must humiliate himself in preparation for his sudden blaze. He must appear to neglect his royal responsibilities, must fritter his time away in vicious idleness, with criminals and drunks, until the moment comes. Like Kim Philby in our own time, he has proposed to himself a life of systematic duplicity; a life of endless conviviality in which he is to have no friend, no possibility of ordinary candour.

The two parts of *Henry IV* probably belong to the years 1596–98, overlapping *The Merchant of Venice*, some two years earlier than *Julius Caesar*, and about six years earlier than *Othello. Coriolanus* may be dated anywhere between 1605 and 1608. In each of these plays we have found some notion of cultural evolution. We have already noticed a transformation of the context, a change in England itself at the beginning of *Henry IV*. The England of *Henry IV* is not the England of *Richard II*. While the anointed king was still on the throne, the country itself seemed still partly taken up into the supernatural. Parables, allegories, Eden, Paradise naturally express the character of this island in the older play. But the England of the usurper has been abandoned to the bleak natural order.

But in order to see whether the notion of cultural evolution is present in the two parts of *Henry IV* we must bring Hotspur into the discussion. Hotspur is culturally more primitive than Hal. Auden observes that under the old kings the country had functioned fairly loosely as a set of small baronies, earldoms and the like, in which the dominant loyalties were local, personal, feudal. This is offered as a statement of a fact available to Shakespeare. A change of mental set, a change in instinctual morality was needed before people learned that their duty to a king they never saw undercut their duty to the man who fed and protected them. It is clear that in Hotspur this change has not occurred.

His energy is half-divine, and his language breathes a freshness which no one else in the play can match. Hal looks at him with a kind of envy— the moral world in which he moves is so simple. At 2.3.1, he enters reading a letter; "He could be contented—why is he not, then?" Hotspur cannot comprehend the hypothetical. Bacon wrote, *antiquitas saeculi, iuventus mundi*, "the age of the ancients was the youth of the world." He was arguing, in a highly guarded fashion, for the moderns against the ancients and brilliantly turned the tables by saying, "If it's age you like you should read the moderns; we are far older than they, who lived in the world's infancy." So Hotspur, who belongs to the old order, is above all young. When he receives his death-wound from the prince he cries,

> O Harry, thou hast robb'd me of my youth.
> (*1 Henry IV* 5.4.77)

Responsibility, prudence, caution, strategy mean nothing to him. Honour is his watchword and honour means fighting, with a complete disregard of personal safety or the probability of victory. Only at the end, when his last battle is impending, does Hotspur begin to think (the measured, bitter reply to Blunt in 4.3 brings the change of style which marks the change of heart). Shakespeare brilliantly makes him wish (at 5.2.48) that only he and Hal might fight that day. Here Hotspur's impetuosity is fused for a moment with pity for the other victims of war. But impetuous he remains. At the end of 5.2 he will not stay to read the letters brought by the messenger. The king wishes his son were like Hotspur, but it would have been disastrous if he had been. Prince Hal is like Virgil's Aeneas in that he is burdened with a sense of history and the crushing obligations implied by the likely succession of events. Aeneas has his Hotspur in Turnus, the young, impetuous leader of the Latins. For both Aeneas and Prince Hal the most important relationships are lineal. Each is dominated by the idea of his father, by Anchises and by the king. Thus for Aeneas the lateral relation with Dido is a distraction which must be crushed.

Here, it may be thought, the analogy breaks down. Hal has no Dido, no mirror love to bear him from his purpose; in the sequence from *Part 1* of *Henry IV* to *Henry V* we have no tragic queen who dies of a broken heart.

Yet someone (if we can believe Pistol, and I think we can) lay dying of a heart "fracted and corroborate" (*Henry V* 2.1.121). The analogy with the *Aeneid* is indeed broken by an explosion of genius, yet at the same time in a manner sustained. We have come back to Falstaff. For Shakespeare has chosen to give us something hilarious: a Dido in the form of an Anchises. The great distracting love of *Henry IV* is an old man, and he drinks.

Falstaff is not like Hotspur a specimen of an earlier culture. Rather, he spans and sums in his person all change, all shocks. He is as Arthurian as he is Henrician, as Arcadian as he is English, paradisal and fallen. Introduced in *Part 1* as irrelevant to clocks ("What a devil has thou to do with the time of day?" says the prince at 1.2.7), he is, as we learn in *Part 2*, soon to die. He is an old man but he is also a sort of timeless baby. The Hostess's account of the death of Falstaff is a wonderful description of a baby: "I saw him fumble with the sheets, and play with flowers, and smile upon his finger's end" (*Henry V* 2.3.15). There is a point when the two images are held in separation, and then glimmer and join. Falstaff says, "I was born about three of the clock in the afternoon, with a white head and something a round belly" (*2 Henry IV* 1.2.176–77). We hear the words and, as we listen, what do we see? A white head and a round belly.

Sublimely Ridiculous:
The Wife of Bath and Falstaff

E. Talbot Donaldson

We can never ascertain whether Shakespeare had the Wife of Bath in mind—at least in his unconscious mind—when he created Falstaff. It may be merely a coincidence that Falstaff in one of his early appearances is seen on the pilgrim route to Canterbury; and it may have been merely Shakespeare's instinct that told him that a gross solipsist of enormous vitality would be the proper comic figure to provide an anti-heroic foil for a fledgling monarch and an ironic commentary on the values of English power politics, and that he never thought of that earlier large solipsist of enormous vitality who provides a foil for all the virtuous wives in fact and fiction and an ironic commentary on the Middle Ages' received ideas about marriage and the nature of women. The ironic commentaries that Falstaff and the Wife of Bath make are, because of the assurance and authority of their personalities, as persuasive as is the reality of the milieus in which they live and to which they respond. Both are supremely self-confident in their idiosyncrasy. As is often pointed out, they both use—or rather misuse—in their own defense the verse of St. Paul in the first Epistle to the Corinthians, in which he enjoins Christ's followers to remain in that vocation to which they have been called. Speaking of her total dedication to the vocation of matrimony, the Wife announces

> In such a state as god hath cleped vs
> I wol perseuer: I nam not precious.
>
> (D 147–48)

From *The Swan at the Well: Shakespeare Reading Chaucer*. © 1985 by Yale University. Yale University Press, 1985.

And when the prince comments on Falstaff's role as a taker of purses, Falstaff replies, "Why, Hal, 'tis my vocation, Hal, 'tis no sin for a man to labor in his vocation." (1.2.104–5). I am not suggesting that Shakespeare needed the Wife of Bath to put St. Paul's text into Falstaff's mind, for the verse from the Epistle is one of several Pauline texts that were probably often perverted in a way that would have terrified the Apostle. In the C-text of *Piers Plowman*, for example, Long Will beats off an attack by Conscience and Reason on his begging for bread for a living by citing the verse as an excuse for not performing manual labor. All three characters are suggesting, with varying degrees of seriousness, that, although others may find what they do reprehensible, they find their occupations fully justified because they are *their* occupations, and they find them congenial. Their ideas of the world may be at variance with other people's ideas, but they are at home with them, and do not intend to alter their styles for anyone. And, if I may pervert Scripture myself, they speak not as the Scribes and Pharisees, but as those having authority.

Judith Kollmann has recently pointed out a number of similarities between *The Canterbury Tales* and *The Merry Wives of Windsor*, and I myself wonder if that play does not make a backhanded acknowledgment of Shakespeare's awareness of *The Wife of Bath*. The merry wives are in many ways, not including wifely virtue, like the Wife of Bath—independent, resourceful, sturdy women of the same middle-class background as she. This is, indeed, as Professor Kollmann shows, a background one associates with Chaucer's *Canterbury Tales* and hardly at all with Shakespeare's plays, which are mostly aristocratic or upper class, with bits of low life thrown in for spice. But the community of Windsor is made up of the same sort of people as the community of the Canterbury pilgrims, and is complete with the Host of the Garter Inn, whose involvement with what is going on around him is like that of the Host of the Tabard Inn, who leads the Canterbury pilgrims. The two wives of the play administer sorely needed lessons about women to two men, a jealous husband and an unlikely lover, and this is an enterprise that the Wife of Bath would have cheered them on in, especially when they punished that most porcine of male chauvinist pigs, Sir John Falstaff, who had the gall to rival her in comic grandeur. And indeed, the punishment of Falstaff is effected by facsimiles of those very fairies whom the Wife of Bath tells us the Friar has blessed out of existence—one of whom teaches a lesson about women to the young rapist in *The Wife of Bath's Tale*.

Of the many traits the Wife of Bath and Falstaff share, one of the most striking is their wit. Of Falstaff, who boasts that the brain of man "is not able to invent anything that intends to laughter more than I invent or is invented upon me," and that he is "not only witty in [him]self, but the cause that wit is in other men" (*Henry IV, Part 2* 1.2.7–10), no more need be said—though it's tempting to say it anyhow. But the Wife's wit is sometimes underestimated. She is, for instance, a past-mistress of the progressively engulfing squelch, the insult that hurts the victim more the more he thinks about it. At the end of a tirade directed at one of her doddering husbands she asks him, out of the blue, "What aileth soche an old man for to chide?" (D 281). Perhaps one has to be a man of advanced—or advancing—years really to feel how this question goes on subtly cutting deeper after the first superficial wound has been felt: apparently old age cancels a man's right to complain about anything, especially a vigorous wife, for an old man ought, she implies, to feel nothing but gratitude for being allowed to clutter up the house with his useless carcass. One does not have to be a friar to savor the wit of her devastating repayment of the Friar on the pilgrimage for his patronizing comments on her learning and the length of her prologue. She explains that the friars, having blessed fairies out of existence, have taken their place: the result is that women may walk the countryside safely, for where there used to be an incubus there is now only a friar, and he'll do nothing to women—except dishonor them (857–81).

As the quotation from St. Paul suggests, both the Wife of Bath and Falstaff are adept at converting received *dicta*, whether biblical or proverbial, into slightly askew statements critical of other people's values or expressive of their own. I say "converting," for the process is not really one of twisting such texts as it is reinterpreting them by a surprising use of logic. That human flesh is frail is an observation so trite that it has lost its force as a moral warning and has become an extenuating statement. Or so Falstaff suggests when he restates it in the comparative degree: "Thou seest I have more flesh than another man, and therefore more frailty" (*Henry I, Part 1,* 3.3.166–68). "The lion will not touch the prince" is a statement which, under Falstaff's analysis, serves to excuse Falstaff's unlion-like failure to oppose Hal and Poins when they rob him of the booty of the Gadshill theft, and also to validate both Hal's claim to be a true prince and Falstaff's to be a lion, whose instinct caused him to run away from his sovereign (2.4.270–75). The Wife of Bath, though her *forte* is the Bible—to which I shall return—matches this refurbishment of an adage by her reinterpretation of the innocent little saying that it is too miserly for a man to refuse to let another man light a candle at his lantern, since he'll have none the less light as a result (D 333–34). When the Wife identifies the man as a husband and the lantern as his wife, the proverb takes on shocking implications, managing to justify a wife's extramarital sexual activity while dutifully preserving the medieval tenet that the wife is the husband's chattel, like any other of his tangible goods.

The Wife of Bath and Falstaff create their individual versions of reality by the protraction of their speech: they erect large verbal structures which fill the listener's mind and exclude from it all other matter. The prologue to the Wife's tale is approximately as long as the Prologue to *The Canterbury Tales*, a proportionment in which she would have found nothing to criticize. In all three of the plays in which Falstaff appears one finds long, long prose passages spoken by Falstaff, sometimes to someone else, but more often to himself, and us. He is a soliloquist more copious than Hamlet. Yet despite the fact that these solipsistic monologists are constantly explaining themselves to us, we are often not sure where to have them. Both make ironic commentaries on their milieus, but both also *are* ironic commentaries on their milieus, and as such they share, along with irony, the effect of making the reader uncertain of the exact locus from which their speeches proceed— their *locus loquendi* if I may invent a critical term. Sturdy no-nonsense commonsense is the basis for one of their guises, though this can at any time modulate into almost frightening sophistication. And both guises can suddenly give way to childlike naiveté—the kind of thing that enables the child in the old story to see that the emperor has no clothes on. And occasionally both seem genuinely naive, becoming parodies of adult behavior in the same way that small children are. One might say that the Wife of Bath and Falstaff share a Wordsworthian child's vision, uncluttered by conventions, with intimations of immorality. And each has a fourth guise as well, though one they do not share: the Wife's is the ferocious aggressive intensity of the shrew, while Falstaff's, rather surprisingly, is that of injured innocence.

Chaucer is careful to confirm our impression of the Wife of Bath's instability of guise when, after the Pardoner's interruption, she consents to his request that she teach him about marriage with an apology, which under the color of clarification produces obfuscation:

> . . . I pray to al this company
> If that I speke after my fantasy
> As taketh not agrefe of that I say,
> For mine entent is not but to playe.
> (D 189–92)

We know precisely what the meanings of the word *fantasy* are, but unfortunately we do not know which of the two dominant meanings is the right one. Serious scholars—over-serious, in my opinion—have suggested that she means by *fantasy* imagination, not delight and, hence, that the whole story of her marriages is a fabrication, just as she tells us that her version of what her old husbands used to say to her when they came home drunk is a fabrication. But to deny that the Wife's account of her marriages is true is to raise the insuperable problem of evaluating the truth of a fiction in relation to the truth of a fiction within a fiction. Are the separate stories in *Don Quixote* more or less true than the story of *Don Quixote*? And, in order to complicate matters, the Wife does not quite say that she is speaking after her fantasy, but asks her hearers not to be offended *if* she speaks after her fantasy: we do not know when, if ever, the protasis of the conditional sentence begins to govern the discourse. Chaucer has been careful to give the Wife of Bath's ironies an elusiveness that makes them seem to be in perpetual motion.

The Wife tells us that her intent is only to play, and that is perhaps true most of the time of Falstaff. But as with the Wife, we are often unsure where his play begins or leaves off. The most obvious example is at the tavern after the Gadshill robbery. When Falstaff boasts of his heroic behavior, and in doing so multiplies two rogues in buckram suits into eleven and then adds three misbegotten knaves in Kendall green (2.4.191–224), does he really expect the prince and Poins to believe him? Actually, the question is easily answered, but answered, unhappily, as easily in the negative as in the affirmative. For Falstaff's expectations are as obscure as those of Chaucer's Pardoner, when, after fully exposing his fraudulence, he tries at the end of his tale to get the Host to buy some of his pardon (C 919–59). Critical argument is unending about whether the Pardoner really thought he could make a sale. The Host's furious response reflects his ill ease, because the Pardoner is a user and exemplifier of irony whose center the Host cannot locate. The reader is apt to be similarly ill at ease with Falstaff, and critics occasionally imitate the Host's treatment of the Pardoner by trying to reduce Falstaff's various guise to mere matter, and to gross matter at that. In a way, that is what Hal is forced to do when he finally rejects Falstaff. He did not overhear Falstaff's catechism on honor at Shrewsbury (5.1.129–41), but as king he would recognize that such playful subversions are more dangerous to his rule than any robberies at Gadshill, despite, or perhaps because of, the catechism's taking the elementary form of a schoolboy's lesson. Such an ambiguously motivated question of Falstaff's when he learns that the party they are about to rob at Gadshill consists of eight or ten men, as "Zounds, will they not rob us?" (2.2.65) may appear on the printed page as pure play. But spoken, it develops ambiguity. Should one say, "Will they not *rob* us?" like an honest man fearing to fall among thieves, or "Will *they* not rob *us*?" like a thief recognizing that there may be other thieves with superior numbers?

And what is one to make—and what did Hal make?—of Falstaff's soliloquy just before the robbery, which is overheard by the prince?

> Well, I doubt not but to die a fair death for all this, if I scape hanging for killing that rogue [Prince Hal]. I have forsworn his company hourly any time this two and twenty years, and yet I am bewitch'd with the rogue's company. If the rascal have not given me medicines to make me love him, I'll be hanged. It could not be else, I have drunk medicines.
>
> [2.2.13–20]

In order to put a consistently cynical and knowing base under Falstaff so he can be pinned down, critics have suggested that he knows Prince Hal is listening, and that he is saying what will ingratiate himself with him. But this is to explain a mystery by denying its existence. It is really another irony that the love of Falstaff for the prince is real, though it is expressed here at once with a childlike naiveté and in the ironical language Falstaff often uses in public, with the reason for his love being assigned to, even blamed on, the prince, a rogue who he feels has corrupted him. Is there some chance that the "reverent vice," as the prince calls him, really has a heart that is suitable for a "goodly portly man, i' faith, and a corpulent, of a cheerful look, a pleasing eye, and a most noble carriage" (2.4.421–23) as Falstaff describes himself? Perhaps.

The Wife of Bath's bases are equally troublesome. Her approach to the Bible and its commentators is a combination of naive literalism, a somewhat questioning sense of reverence, and plain common sense grounded in experience. She has trouble, as moralistic critics are always pointing out, understanding that it is not the letter but the spirit that one must heed. The relevant significance of Christ's remark to the Samaritan women at the well, "Thou hast had five husbands and that man that now hath thee is not thy husband" (D 14–25), eludes her. And well is might. The proposition, of which she has been told, that the text somehow limits the number of husbands a woman can have to five (six being over the legal limit) stems from St. Jerome, who heaped his Pelion of antifeminism upon the antifeminist Ossa of St. Paul. St. Jerome's proposition was based on his misreading of the biblical story, a confusion worse confounded by the Wife when she fails to understand that Christ was referring not to a fifth husband, but to a sixth man to whom the Samaritan woman had said she was not married—a disclaimer suppressed by St. Jerome in his eagerness to see that his reading of the spirit should not be belied by the letter. The tenuousness of such blatantly prejudiced spiritual readings of the Bible is equally reflected in the Wife of Bath's natural perplexity and the saint's willful inaccuracy. The absurdity is enhanced by the Wife's attempt to fit the proposition to herself by misreading St. Jerome's misreading, so that the number of husbands comes out to four plus one questionable one, instead of five plus one man unwedded. Five is her current total if, as she carefully says, the fifth was canonically legal. But she herself can think of no explanation for Christ's choice of the number four, and seems ultimately to decide that the number of consecutive husbands she may have is unlimited.

In dealing with St. Paul, the Wife uses a literalist approach worthy of a puritan reformer. She reminds him of his admission that on the subject of matrimony he had no higher authority (79–82). And she uses those texts that please her and lets the others go without notice. She knows that her husband should leave father and mother and take only unto her (30–31), and that she has power over her husband's body and not he (158–59), but she fails to mention any reciprocal obligation. Yet in so doing she is providing a naturally ironic commentary on generations of celibate experts on marriage, who endlessly repeat the woman's obligation and rarely mention the husband's. She is understandably uncertain why, if the patriarchs had a number of wives, multiplicity of spouses is now deemed reprehensible (55–58). She envies Solomon his many spouses, and suppresses—if she is aware of it—the fact that Solomon's uxoriousness in building temples to his wives' strange gods brought the Lord's wrath down on him (35–43).

She even performs a bit of sophisticated biblical interpretation of her own: first she wishes that she had Solomon's gift from God of being "refreshed" by spouses as often as he was (37–38); later she remarks that she is willing to let virgins be bread of pure wheat seed and wives barley bread; but finally she notes that with barley bread Christ "refreshed" many a man (143–46)—a mixture of letter and spirit that would do credit to a patristic, intellectually speaking, if not morally. Her culminating combining of simplicity and sophistication occurs in her lament, "Alas, alas, that euer loue was sin!" (614). Moralists sometimes seize on this as proof that the Wife was aware of her sinfulness and regretted it. But her apparent repentance is actually parody, a parody of the repentance one is led to expect. It is not Christian remorse that provokes her exclamation, but regret that because sexual love is sin its availability to her has been reduced. An old age of repentance is no more the Wife of Bath's prospectus than it ever was Falstaff's.

Both the Wife of Bath and Falstaff are, though utterly charming, perfectly horrible people. It is true that the Wife's victims are mostly husbands who deserved the abuse and exploitation she practiced on them. But she is a habitual fornicator and adulterer, and her ability to be disagreeable when her authority is challenged is not limited to the domestic scene, as any parish wife who gets to the Offering before her learns. Falstaff is not only a drunken old man, but a thief, a deadbeat, an exploiter of poor women and shallow justices from whom he borrows money that he fails to repay, an abuser of the king's press, a lecher, a liar, and heaven knows what else. And as two very dubious citizens, they should *not* be sentimentalized. I say this very sternly, for I am aware that I can never discuss them at length without sentimentalizing them. I blame this on their creators, who seem to have loved them dearly while endowing them with enough vices to supply an army of the wicked—enough vices and enough vitality. I have always supposed that *Henry IV Part 2* exists largely because Falstaff's vitality was too bountiful to be confined in *Part 1*; and surely *The Merry Wives of Windsor* exists because of him. Shakespeare originally promised that Falstaff would show up in *Henry V* (Epilogue to *Henry IV, Part 2*), but prudently changed his mind and killed him off before he could stop Hal from ever getting to Agincourt. The Wife of Bath managed to get herself into *The Merchant's Tale* (E 1685–87) and into Chaucer's "Envoy to Bukton"—also an unruly fiction who would not remain on the page where she belonged. Both characters took on life independent of their creators.

And both are associated with passages of unrivaled emotional effectiveness, passages that are as splendid tributes to human vitality as any I know. The Wife of Bath speaks hers, and Falstaff's is spoken about him. The Wife of Bath's is a digression from her account of her fourth husband:

> My fourth husbonde was a reuelour—
> That is to saie, he had a paramour.
> And I was yong, and full of ragerie,
> Stubburne and strong, and ioly as a Pie.
> Well coud I daunce to an Harpe smale,
> And sing, iwis, as a Nitingale,
> Whan I had dronken a draught of swete wine.
> Metellus, the foule churle, the swine,
> That with a staffe biraft his wife her life
> For she dronk wine, though I had be his wife,
> He should not haue daunted me fro drinke.
> And after wine of Venus must I thinke,
> For also seker as cold engendreth haile,

A likorus mouth must haue a lecherous taile.
In women vinolent is no defence:
This knowe lecherous by experience.

But lord Christ, when it remembreth me
Vpon my youth and my iolite,
It tickleth me about the hart roote—
Vnto this daie is doeth my hart boote—
That I haue had my worlde as in my time.
But age, alas, that all woll enuenime
Hath me biraft my beaute and my pith.
Let go, fare well, the deuile go therwith!
The floure is gon, ther nis no more to tell;
The bran, as I best can, now mote I sell.
But yet to be right merie woll I fonde.
Now forth to tell of my fourth husbonde!
[D 453–80]

I doubt that many who have spent their lives far better than the Wife are able to look back with such a sense of benediction as that with which the Wife of Bath looks back on her misspent past. She has enjoyed life, and will go on enjoying it. And although she is a very immoral woman, she has, in her enjoyment, perfect integrity.

Perhaps Falstaff was incapable of so philosophical a looking back— that was not one of his guises. But Shakespeare gives him the same kind of emotional justification in the erstwhile Mistress Quickly's account of his death in *Henry V*, a kind of apology for the dramatist for Hal's shabby treatment of him and the merry wives' triumph over him. In the scene, Bardolph has just reacted violently to Falstaff's death, wishing he were "with him, wheresome'er he is, either in heaven or hell." The Hostess replies:

Nay sure, he's not in hell; he's in Arthur's bosom, if ever man went to Arthur's bosom. 'A made a finer end, and went away and it had been any christom child. 'A parted ev'n just between twelve and one, ev'n at the turning o' th' tide; for after I saw him fumble with the sheets, and play with flowers, and smile upon his finger's end, I knew there was but one way; for his nose was as sharp as a pen, and 'a [talked] of green fields. "How now, Sir John?" quoth I, "what, man? be a' good cheer." So 'a cried out, "God, God, God!" three or four times. Now I, to

comfort him, bid him 'a should not think of God; I hop'd there
was no need to trouble himself with any such thoughts yet. So
'a bade me lay more clothes on his feet. I put my hand into the
bed and felt them, and they were as cold as any stone; then I
felt to his knees, [and they were as cold as any stone;] and so
up'ard and up'ard, and all was as cold as any stone.

Both passages occur in marvelously comic contexts, and both are perfectly
controlled in their tone, with the pathos not spoiling the humor, or vice
versa. I don't think we should worry about the Hostess' misplacement of
Falstaff in Arthur's bosom, any more than we should worry about the final
destination of the Wife of Bath's soul—*she* never did. Both characters are
in any case still very much alive, very much their creator's celebrations of
life, and I can hardly think of anything better to celebrate.

Chronology

1564	William Shakespeare born at Stratford-on-Avon to John Shakespeare, a butcher, and Mary Arden. He is baptized on April 26.
1582	Marries Anne Hathaway in November.
1583	Daughter Susanna born, baptized on May 26.
1585	Twins Hamnet and Judith born, baptized on February 2.
1588–90	Sometime during these years, Shakespeare goes to London, without family. First plays performed in London.
1590–92	*The Comedy of Errors*, the three parts of *Henry VI*.
1593–94	Publication of *Venus and Adonis* and *The Rape of Lucrece*, both dedicated to the Earl of Southampton. Shakespeare becomes a sharer in the Lord Chamberlain's company of actors. *The Taming of the Shrew, The Two Gentlemen of Verona, Richard III*.
1595–97	*Romeo and Juliet, Richard II, King John, A Midsummer Night's Dream, Love's Labor's Lost*.
1596	Son Hamnet dies. Grant of arms to father.
1597	*The Merchant of Venice, Henry IV, Part 1*. Purchases New Place in Stratford.
1598–1600	*Henry IV, Part 2, As You Like It, Much Ado About Nothing, Twelfth Night, The Merry Wives of Windsor, Henry V*, and *Julius Caesar*. Moves his company to the new Globe Theatre.
1601	*Hamlet*. Shakespeare's father dies, buried on September 8.
1603	Death of Queen Elizabeth; James VI of Scotland becomes James I of England; Shakespeare's company becomes the King's Men.
1603–4	*All's Well That Ends Well, Measure for Measure, Othello*.
1605–6	*King Lear, Macbeth*.

1607	Marriage of daughter Susanna on June 5.
1607–8	*Timon of Athens, Antony and Cleopatra, Pericles.*
1608	Shakespeare's mother dies, buried on September 9.
1609	*Cymbeline,* publication of sonnets. Shakespeare's company purchases Blackfriars Theatre.
1610–11	*The Winter's Tale, The Tempest.* Shakespeare retires to Stratford.
1616	Marriage of daughter Judith on February 10. William Shakespeare dies at Stratford on April 23.
1623	Publication of the Folio edition of Shakespeare's plays.

Contributors

HAROLD BLOOM, Sterling Professor of the Humanities at Yale University, is the author of *The Anxiety of Influence, Poetry and Repression,* and many other volumes of literary criticism. His forthcoming study, *Freud: Transference and Authority,* attempts a full-scale reading of all of Freud's major writings. A MacArthur Prize Fellow, he is general editor of five series of literary criticism published by Chelsea House.

HAROLD C. GODDARD was Head of the Department of English at Swarthmore College from 1909 to 1946.

WYNDHAM LEWIS was a novelist, poet, and critic associated with Ezra Pound and the Vorticist Revolution. He is best remembered as the author of *Tarr* and *The Apes of God.*

C. L. BARBER was Professor of Literature at the University of California, Santa Cruz. At the time of his death, he was completing a second book on Shakespeare.

RICARDO QUINONES is Professor of Comparative Literature at Claremont McKenna College and author of *Mapping Literary Modernism: Time and Development.*

MICHAEL MCCANLES is Professor of English at Marquette University and author of *The Discourse of* Il Principe.

ELLIOT KRIEGER is author of *A Marxist Study of Shakespeare's Comedies.*

DAVID SUNDELSON is Professor of Literature at the California Institute of Technology.

A. D. NUTTALL is Professor of English at the University of Sussex. His books include *A Common Sky* and *A New Mimesis.*

E. TALBOT DONALDSON, Professor Emeritus of English at Indiana University at Bloomington, is our preeminent critic and scholar of Chaucer.

Bibliography

Bamber, Linda. *Comic Women, Tragic Men*. Stanford, Calif.: Stanford University Press, 1982.

Battenhouse, Roy. "Falstaff as Parodist and Perhaps Holy Fool." *PMLA* 90 (1975): 32–52.

Bergeron, David M., ed. *Pageantry in the Shakespearean Theater*. Athens: University of Georgia Press, 1986.

Blanpied, John. *Time and the Artist in Shakespeare's History Plays*. Newark: University of Delaware Press, 1983.

Calderwood, James. *Metadrama in Shakespeare's Henriad*. Berkeley: University of California Press, 1979.

Campbell, Lily Bess. *Shakespeare's "Histories": Mirrors of Elizabethan Policy*. San Marino, Calif.: Huntington Library, 1947.

Dean, Leonard, *"Richard II* to *Henry V:* A Closer View." In *Studies in Honor of De Witt T. Starnes,* edited by Thomas P. Harrison et al. Austin: University of Texas Press, 1967.

Dorius, R. J. *Twentieth Century Interpretations of* Henry IV, Part One: *A Collection of Critical Essays*. Englewood Cliffs, N.J.: Prentice-Hall, 1970.

Eastman, Arthur M. *A Short History of Shakespearean Criticism*. New York: W. W. Norton and Co., 1968.

Empson, William. "Falstaff and Mr. Dover Wilson." *Kenyon Review* 15, no. 2 (Spring 1953): 213–62.

Erickson, Peter, and Coppélia Kahn, eds. *Shakespeare's "Rough Magic": Renaissance Essays in Honor of C. L. Barber*. Newark: University of Delaware Press, 1986.

Faber, M. D. "Falstaff Behind the Arras." *American Imago* 27, no. 3 (1970): 197–225.

Gottschalk, Paul. "Hal, and the 'Play Extempore' in *1 Henry IV.*" *Texas Studies in Literature and Language* 15 (1974): 604–14.

Hawkins, Harriet. *The Devil's Party: Critical Counterinterpretations of Shakespearean Drama*. Oxford: Oxford University Press, 1986.

Holderness, Graham. *Shakespeare's History*. New York: St. Martin's, 1986.

Hunter, G. K. *The Structural Problem in Shakespeare's* Henry the Fourth. London: Methuen, 1956.

Kernan, Alvin B. *"The Henriad:* Shakespeare's Major History Plays." In *Modern Shakespearean Criticism,* edited by Alvin B. Kernan, 245–75. New York: Harcourt Brace Jovanovich, 1970.

Kris, E. "Prince Hal's Conflict." *Psychoanalytic Quarterly* 17 (1948): 487–506.

Levin, Harry. *Shakespeare and the Revolution of the Times: Perspectives and Commentaries*. Oxford: Oxford University Press, 1976.

McLuhan, Herbert M. "*Henry IV*: A Mirror for Magistrates." *University of Toronto Quarterly* 17 (1947): 152–60.

Manheim, Michael. *The Weak King Dilemma in the Shakespearean History Play*. Syracuse, N.Y.: Syracuse University Press, 1973.

Marienstras, Richard. *New Perspectives on the Shakespearean World*. Cambridge: Cambridge University Press, 1986.

Ornstein, Robert. *A Kingdom for a Stage: The Achievement of Shakespeare's History Plays*. Cambridge: Harvard University Press, 1972.

Pierce, Robert B. *Shakespeare's History Plays: The Family and the State*. Columbus: Ohio State University Press, 1971.

Prior, Moody E. *The Drama of Power: Studies in Shakespeare's History Plays*. Evanston, Ill.: Northwestern University Press, 1973.

Reese, M. M. *The Cease of Majesty: A Study of Shakespeare's History Plays*. London: Methuen, 1961.

Ribner, Irving. *The English History Play in the Age of Shakespeare*. Princeton: Princeton University Press, 1957.

Richmond, Hugh M. *Shakespeare's Political Plays*. New York: Random House, 1962.

Rossiter, A. P. "Ambivalence: The Dialectic of the Histories." In *Angel With Horns*. New York: Longmans, 1969.

Saccio, Peter. *Shakespeare's English Kings*. London: Oxford University Press, 1977.

Sanders, Wilbur. *The Dramatist and the Received Idea*. London: Cambridge University Press, 1968.

Schuchter, J. D. "Prince Hal and Francis: The Imitation of an Action." *Shakespeare Studies* 3 (1967): 129–37.

Smidt, Kristian. *Unconformities in Shakespeare's History Plays*. London: Macmillan, 1982.

Stoll, Elmer Edgar. *Shakespeare Studies*. New York: Macmillan, 1927.

Thayer, C. G. *Shakespearean Politics: Government and Misgovernment in the Great Histories*. Athens: Ohio University Press, 1983.

Tillyard, E. M. W. *Shakespeare's History Plays*. London: Chatto & Windus, 1944.

Traversi, Derek A. *Shakespeare from* Richard II *to* Henry IV. Stanford, Calif.: Stanford University Press, 1957.

Watson, Robert N. *Shakespeare and the Hazards of Ambition*. Cambridge: Harvard University Press, 1984.

Webber, Joan. "The Renewal of the King's Symbolic Role: From *Richard II* to *Henry V*." *Texas Studies in Literature and Language* 4 (1963): 530–38.

Wells, Stanley. *Shakespeare: An Illustrated Dictionary*. Oxford: Oxford University Press, 1986.

Wilders, John. *The Lost Garden*. London: Macmillan, 1978.

Wilson, J. Dover. *The Fortunes of Falstaff*. New York: Macmillan, 1944.

Wilson, J. Dover, and T. C. Worsley. *Shakespeare's Histories at Stratford, 1951*. London: M. Reinhardt, 1952.

Winny, James. *The Player King: A Theme of Shakespeare's Histories*. New York: Barnes & Noble, 1968.

Acknowledgments

"Henry IV" by Harold C. Goddard from *The Meaning of Shakespeare* by Harold C. Goddard, © 1951 by The University of Chicago. Reprinted by permission of the University of Chicago Press.

"Falstaff and Don Quixote" by Wyndham Lewis from *The Lion and the Fox* by Wyndham Lewis, © 1951 and 1955 by Harper and Brothers Publishers. Reprinted by permission.

"Rule and Misrule in *Henry IV, Part 1*" (originally entitled "Rule and Misrule in *Henry IV*") by C. L. Barber from *Shakespeare's Festive Comedies: A Study of Dramatic Form and Its Relation to Social Custom* by C. L. Barber, © 1959 by Princeton University Press. Reprinted by permission.

"The Growth of Hal" (originally entitled "Shakespeare's Histories") by Ricardo J. Quinones from *The Renaissance Discovery of Time* by Ricardo J. Quinones, © 1972 by the President and Fellows of Harvard College. Reprinted by permission of Harvard University Press.

"The Dialectic of Right and Power in *Henry IV, Part 1*" (originally entitled "The Dialectic of Right and Power in Eight Plays of Shakespeare, 1595–1604") by Michael McCanles from *Dialectical Criticism and Renaissance Literature* by Michael McCanles, © 1975 by the Regents of the University of California. Reprinted by permission of the University of California Press.

" 'To Demand the Time of Day': Prince Hal" (originally entitled *"Henry IV, Part One"*) by Elliot Krieger from *A Marxist Study of Shakespeare's Comedies* by Elliot Krieger, © 1979 by Elliot Krieger. Reprinted by permission of Macmillan Press Ltd. and Barnes and Noble Books.

"Prince Hal's Joke" (originally entitled "Fathers, Sons and Brothers in the *Henriad*") by David Sundelson from *Shakespeare's Restoration of the Father* by David Sundelson, © 1983 by Rutgers, The State University. Reprinted by permission of Rutgers University Press.

Index